THE PRIVATION

Fire Ant Books

YOURS FRATERNALLY,

MARCUS B. TONEY,

COMPANY B, CONFEDERATE VETERANS, FIRST REGIMENT
STATE GUARDS, TENNESSEE.

THE PRIVATIONS
OF A PRIVATE

*Campaigning with the First Tennessee,
C. S. A., and Life Thereafter*

Marcus B. Toney

With a New Introduction by Robert E. Hunt
and a New Index

The University of Alabama Press
Tuscaloosa

Introduction copyright © 2005
The University of Alabama Press
Tuscaloosa, Alabama 35487–0380
All rights reserved

Manufactured in the United States of America

∞

The paper on which this book is printed meets the minimum
requirements of American National Standard for Information
Science—Permanence of Paper for Printed Library Materials,
ANSI Z39.48–1984.

CONTENTS

CHAPTER VIII.

CHAPTER IX.

CHAPTER X.

CHAPTER XI.

CHAPTER XII.

CHAPTER XIII.

INTRODUCTION TO
THE PRIVATIONS OF A PRIVATE

Many readers of this volume will be familiar with Sam
Watkins's *"Co. Aytch."* His stirring combat narrative
has for years been the delight of Confederate history
enthusiasts and Civil War buffs alike, and Ken Burns has
cemented Watkins's character in the minds of the main-
stream television audience by using sizeable portions
of *"Co. Aytch"* in his Civil War series. In the face of this
fame and prominence, Marcus B. Toney's *Privations of
a Private* will read like a memoir from a different war.
Although the two men served in the same regiment—
the First Tennessee Infantry—their remembrances run
in very different directions. In part, this is due to the
fact that the two men *actually had* disparate experiences.
Marcus Toney spent a good deal of the war as a POW,
and, compared to Watkins, saw a relatively small amount
of combat. Yet, readers familiar with *"Co. Aytch"* will
readily see that *Privations* is distinct by intent. Toney
had an endgame very different from his comrade.

Certainly, like Watkins, Toney wanted to compose
an account of the Confederate war. As the title *Privations of a Private* suggests, he wanted to convey the
hardships faced by Southern soldiers, particularly by
those who served time in prison camps. In this respect,
Toney's work fits well within the norm of Lost Cause

chronicles that glorify the steadfastness of the men in gray, and which refuse to apologize for secession. Yet, in contrast to *"Co. Aytch,"* and to many other Southern narratives, Toney focuses on more than the fighting. In *Privations,* the war is no island. Toney refuses to confine Confederate history to the battlefield, or to limit his South to generals and charging men. Indeed, as the reader will see, Marcus Toney does next to nothing with combat narrative and rather sneers at soldiering. He has little use for the army. The major reason for this is that Toney sought to widen the discussion. For him, the issues of the Confederate war included the prewar debate over slavery, Reconstruction, the Ku Klux Klan, and the modernization of the South. In other words, in *Privations,* the war is one event within a larger context of nineteenth- and early twentieth–century history.

Marcus Toney is very clear that he not only wants to defend Southern actions on the eve of the war but to make the Confederate republic relevant to postwar developments. In his eyes, defeating the Southern in-dependence movement did not in any way destroy the Confederacy's mission, and it is the author's joy that turn-of-the-century America had apparently seen fit to recognize the fact. In *Privations,* Toney does not defend a lost and lamented Old South; he lauds the sacred ideals of a South made important again. *Privations* reveals an author passionately convinced of his region's significance for the industrial age. For this resi-dent of turn-of-the-century Nashville, the war did not seal the plantation regime into some romantic Twelve

Oaks nostalgia, nor, in contrast to Watkins, did it box up the South into a definitive but isolated moment of glorious war. Rather, the Cotton Kingdom, the Confederate republic, Reconstruction, and the railroad era all fit into one continuous, if bumpy, history. As Toney puts it, by 1900 his region stood vindicated "not [as] the new South, but the old South, with new life infused into it."[1]

The author was well situated to undertake an effort to link Old South and New. He was born in Campbell County, Virginia in August of 1840, the son of William Henry Clay Toney and Elizabeth Ann Minton Goodwin. Both parents were originally from the Old Dominion, the Goodwin family tracing itself back to 1616. The elder Toney was a significant tradesman: a wheelwright, millwright, and carpenter, according to what Marcus later described. In keeping with the rootlessness of the Jacksonian age, the family moved west in 1842, perhaps in response to the country's unsettled fortunes during the Panic of 1837. They intended to go to St. Louis, but located in Nashville because the Cumberland river was low, and because of Elizabeth's health. Marcus later described her as frail, and without question her life was tragic. She would lose three of the four children born to her, and would die herself in 1846.[2]

Two years after their move, William had crossed the river to the little settlement of Edgefield, buying ten acres and establishing a saw and grist mill. The 1850 census listed the father as a carpenter, though Marcus later stated that he was such "only on his own premises. He did not work for other people." By this census year, he had become a farmer in addition to being a miller, with 30 acres of improved land (plus 20 acres un-improved), raising corn, oats, pigs, and other assorted foodstuffs and barnyard animals.[3]

Significantly, the elder Toney owned slaves: Thirty-five by Marcus's count. Of these persons, most or all had to have been skilled workers of some sort. Not only did the son later note that the father built a four-room house with "his slaves who were carpenters," he reported that only three of the thirty-five actually worked on the estate. William "hired out the others." The father, in short, was a labor broker, most likely of skilled or semi-skilled workmen (and women?), taking advantage of the growth of Nashville as a commercial center.[4]

His father's varied occupations gave the younger Toney an intriguing take on the "peculiar institution." As evidenced by his memoir, Toney completely supported slavery as a racially and economically benevolent insti-tution. Yet, in a questionnaire given to Tennessee's sur-viving Civil War veterans during the World War I era, the ex-Confederate hinted at certain problems of class caused by the system. In answer to a question about whether there were opportunities "for a poor young man—honest and industrious—to save up enough money to buy a small farm or go into business," Toney replied, "yes, at work in cities, but it would take him a long time on the farm against slave labor." In answer to another question about whether slave owners would "mingle freely with those who did not own slaves," the ex-soldier observed that "the slave owners were a class unto themselves." Elsewhere, Toney noted that while not "antagonistic" to those below them on the social ladder, "the slave owners were aloof."[5]

Intriguingly, in answering these questions, it is never quite clear whether Toney includes his own family among the ranks of slave owners, or whether he means a planter class apart from them. In the answer to one question, he distinctly refers to "we" in his discussion of those who held slaves, but in every other response it reads as though he is describing a group well outside his own. At the very least, if he intended to include his own family among those he defines as the ownership class, his remarks were not particularly flattering.

All this suggests that Toney and his family were people wedged into something of an "other" category in regards to the plantation-driven Old South. As an artisan-business family, the Toneys were in no sense part of the agrarian gentry. There was no big house, no village of quarters, no acres of cotton, no rural myth. Yet, the father was certainly utilizing the slave system to carve his slice from the Jacksonian economic pie. Unfortunately, we do not know who these hired slaves were or what enterprises they found themselves in. We do not know if they jobbed on the side, lived apart from the Toneys, or in other ways created space and competency for themselves beyond the master, as other slaves did in the hire-out system. We do know that young Marcus grew up in that part of the "peculiar institution" known for its dynamism and its merging with the coming industrial world.[6]

But the boy would find his childhood cut short. Elizabeth Goodwin died in 1846, just four years after the Toneys moved to Nashville. Then, William died in 1852—while Marcus was "a mere lad," he later said. Suddenly, this youngster who had already lost three siblings and a mother found himself an orphan. Family moved him back to Virginia, where he ended up in college near Lynchburg. He returned to Nashville in 1860 to clerk on a steamboat and lived, apparently, in the family's old house in Edgefield. Then, the young man, not quite twenty-one, found himself in the middle of America's most important war, as he describes in *Privations*.[7]

After being held in prison camp in Elmira, New York during the war's last two years, Toney returned home in the summer of 1865 to unstable times. The Nashville city directory lists him in different occupations year by year, including 1869, when it appears that he was either running the business or acting as a principal agent for the House Furnishing Emporium, selling silver-plated ware and Queensware. During this period he boarded at various locations, moving nearly once a year. During 1870, he boarded at a Mrs. Claiborne's, at 77 Broad Street, which may be significant for the fact that, in 1872, he married one Sally Hill Claiborne. That same year, Toney's life began to settle in other ways. He became a freight agent for the Merchant's Dispatch Company, handling business and traffic for New York Central Railroad system. He would remain with this firm for forty years.[8] The former Confederate soldier became part of the railroad age in the most literal sense, in the process earning the praise of at least one compendium of Tennessee men of business. According to the *History of Tennessee and Tennesseans,* Toney's "responsibilities have increased in proportion as the commerce and transportation of the nation have expanded in these four decades." "Mr. Toney," the compendium noted, "possesses the faculty of being able to adapt himself to the changing conditions of a growing business, and has rendered a valuable service both to his corporation and the public."[9]

Yet, as Toney became a successful man of the New South, he never left the Confederate memory behind. Beginning well before the Lost Cause became a movement, the ex-soldier developed a lecture in 1877 on his POW experiences, "Prison Life in the North," which he gave in various venues over the years.[10] Then, when Nashville became one of the centers of the Confederate memory industry—due to the efforts of Sumner A. Cunningham and his *Confederate Veteran* magazine— Toney was on the ground floor of the enterprise. In the very first issue of the *Veteran,* January 1893, Sally Toney is noted as being on the general committee to raise funds for monuments in Richmond. Toney himself appears frequently in the *Veteran*'s pages as the writer of anecdotal stories or in conjunction with some commemorative activity. As his memoir makes clear, Toney knew Cunningham himself, as the two attended a memorial service for the Confederate dead in Northern prisons. He became enough of a fixture in the Lost Cause movement that a tree was planted in his honor at the Tennessee Soldiers' Home.[11]

It is clear from Toney's memoir that his active involvement in the cause of remembering was anything but nostalgic, and in no way focused on the war in isolation. In this, *Privations* stands in marked contrast to *"Co. Aytch."* In Sam Watkins's famous work, the original causes of the war and its larger meaning are left dim.

Indeed, the Columbia, Tennessee resident constructs the image of a thoughtless war, of a Southern people moved by a sectionalist dream that was, from its infancy, an impossible foolishness. William L. Yancey, the famous secessionist, advocated "a strange and peculiar notion," Watkins says, to divide North from South. "Everybody knew at the time," he continues, "that it was but the idiosyncrasy of an unbalanced mind, and that the United States of America had no north, no south, no east, no west." Aggressive sectionalism, in other words, was pure unreason, "absurd, ridiculous and preposterous." As Watkins notes later in the volume, "'*We are one and undivided.*'"[12]

In one respect, Watkins was flirting here with a war-guilt clause. He was all but accusing his region's political leaders of starting a needless war over an impossible ideological fantasy. It is a mite risky for the losers to chalk up the deaths of 620,000 people to a mere idiosyncrasy of an unbalanced mind. Yet, the effect and the intent of his prose is to strip away the politics of causes and issues. By trivializing sectionalism, he removes any larger meaning or agenda from it, confining it to an easily jettisoned drift into unreason. He isolates and abstracts the war, which, in turn, allows him to pursue his real object: glorifying the Southern fighting man.

The bones of our brave Southern boys lie scattered over our loved South. They fought for their "country," and gave their lives freely for that country's cause; . . . We shed a tear over their flower-strewn graves. We live after them. We love their memory yet. But one generation passes away and another generation follows. We know our loved and brave soldiers. We love them yet.[13]

For his part, Toney was hardly opposed to celebrating the valor of valorous men, but it is clear from *Privations* that he had no wish to do this at the expense of clouding the larger meaning of the war. The politics of the conflict mattered very much. Causes and context were vital: anything but idiosyncratic musing. Indeed, the issues were still current at the turn of the century, in particular the matter of race.

In distinct contrast to Watkins, Toney leaves no doubt about the sectionalist fight that led to secession. No vague ideology of the ridiculous here. The sections diverged because abolitionists like Harriet Beecher Stowe inflamed the slavery question. The tales of horror in *Uncle Tom's Cabin,* Toney argues, slandered a regime in which a race incapable of caring for itself was protected and nurtured. Dangerous libel spurred sectional tensions and the result became separation, he insists. Moreover, in Toney's description, the critical result of the war was not the glorification of the private soldier, but the unwise act of emancipation. Confederate boys, the ex-soldier notes, set off with romantic notions about needing only cornstalks to whip the Yankees, hoping to "return home finding all our servants smiling at our home-coming." Instead, the slaves were free, "but morally and financially in much worse state than when I left them." In *Privations,* the war was all about the disintegration of the racial order.[14]

Toney makes this point vividly in his description of his time as a POW. Held for some weeks at Point Lookout, Maryland, the author and his comrades found themselves guarded by a regiment of African American troops. Disarmed in the presence of these men, Toney reflected that "it was very humiliating to Southern men to be thus guarded by some of their own former slaves." But more than humiliation, there was danger here, for the attitude of the black Union soldiers was menacing and vengeful. "Our ears were frequently greeted with the expression from the colored guards: 'the bottom rail is on top now; my gun wants to smoke.'" Toney then continued soberly, "they were, nearly all of them, young Negroes from the North Carolina tobacco fields. They were uniformed the same as white troops, and of course they felt their importance."[15]

The main theme of the rest of the memoir is the tragic consequences of "bottom rail on top," and the desperate need for the nation to make the situation right again. As the reader will see, Toney argues that things degenerated to the point that vigilantes were required to restore order. The Nashville resident expressly defends the Ku Klux Klan (one of his obituaries identified him as a member), noting that Southerners had been made "slaves to our slaves." Only regional "home rule" and the defeat of Reconstruction resolved the situation. This accomplished, "we were freemen, as the yoke of slavery had been lifted from our necks."[16] In Toney's eyes, the Lost Cause was less a commemoration of the war than a celebration of white supremacy's solid victory in the South and in national politics.

Toney's concentration on race is consistent with others in the Confederate commemoration movement who not only defended the Klan but linked the organization to the soldiers in gray who originally fought for

Southern independence. As in *Privations,* the two fights were seen as essentially the same. Laura Rose, member of the United Daughters of the Confederacy, linked the Confederate army to the hooded order in a 1909 pamphlet intended to support building a monument to Southern veterans in Beauvoir, Mississippi. In addition to her own description, Rose reprinted a letter from J. B. Kennedy, one of the Pulaski, Tennessee founders.

The Ku Klux Klans were composed of the very best citizens of our country; Their mission was to protect the weak and oppressed during the dark days of Reconstruction. To protect the women of the South, who were the loveliest, noblest, and best women in the world. . . . [We] are proud of having worn the gray for four long years, and defending their homes and loved ones.[17]

Rose later authored a more extensive book, *The Ku Klux Klan, or Invisible Empire,* which was endorsed alike by the United Daughters of the Confederacy and the Sons of Confederate Veterans. This was a work intended as a schoolbook for young children, and it contains a dedication intended to inspire the young of the "Southland . . . with respect and admiration for the Confederate soldiers, who were the real Ku Klux, and whose deeds of courage and valor, have never been surpassed."[18] For people like Rose and Toney, celebrating the Confederate war and the restoration of white rule were one and the same thing.

Yet, if recalling the days of "bottom rail on top" was a troubling memory for Toney, it is intriguing that his story of the Klan does not really center on race. If Reconstruction was the *real* war in the author's eyes, then it is odd that he both affirms white over black and diverts from it. As Toney explains it, "we had no law and order; everything was in a chaotic state." The Klan, he goes on, was not organized "especially to intimidate the blacks." "[W]hites as well, if guilty of wrong doing," found themselves visited. "I have always maintained," Toney concludes, "that the Klans were great conservators of law and order." "The blacks who behaved themselves," he insists, "had the best of friends in the Kuklux Klan."[19]

It is easy to sneer at this language, of course, looking back from the distance of a century in time, and from the vantage of the post–Civil Rights era. By all objective accounts, the Ku Klux Klan was a terrorist organization, and Toney's apologies for it seem little less than self-delusion worthy of the United Daughters. From the best available evidence, the Klan in Tennessee was all about the brutal politics of internal civil war. Although the state was never officially reconstructed, it had divided bitterly and violently over secession, particularly in the middle and eastern sections. Unionist occupation of middle Tennessee—a factor since the capture of Nashville in February 1862—had pushed the region into cruel guerilla war and a nasty politics of disfranchisement and arrest. The Reconstruction era simply embedded the racial factor even deeper into this controversy.[20]

In other words, despite what he says, middle Tennessee was not caught in some sort of indiscriminate lawlessness but in a very specific, internal civil war that began before the official fight between North and South commenced and that continued long after Appomattox. Toney's memoir obscures and covers over what was actually a brutal political contest that convulsed Tennessee from the beginning of the secession movement until long past Lee's surrender. Toney's side won and, by the turn of the century, was rewriting the history to follow through. The author's contribution was to dress up a wicked, ugly struggle between secessionists and unionists and transform it into a grand moral contest between the forces of law and anarchy.

Yet, considered in another way, Toney's war between order and chaos may have been more than the usual fabrications of winner's history. From the vantage point of people living at the turn of the century, the previous fifty years could well have seemed to be one convulsion after another. Those of Toney's age had in their memories the full sweep of vicious of civil war, the cruel, hard fight over "bottom rail on top," and the persistent nasty feelings between the sections. Moreover, the new industrial order brought dislocations of its own: immigrant labor, cities and their slums, red light districts, hideous poverty, aggressive, arrogant wealth, and depressions. Indeed, as a railroad agent in Nashville, Toney was alive to this new issue as well. Certainly he expressed his share of cynicism about the age of the robber barons. Commenting on a move to shift the McLean House (where Lee surrendered at Appomattox) to Chicago, along with a re-creation of Richmond's notorious Libby Prison, Toney observed that this move seemed "intended not so much as a monument to the inhumanity of the Southern people as it was to fill some enterprising citizens' pockets with the shekels."[21]

Over and again the theme that emerges from *Privations* is that race subordination was included as part of a larger need to respond to a hydra-headed degeneracy. The theme in the memoir is less the specific politics of the Klan than a more a generalized need for honesty, sincerity, and generosity of spirit. Certainly, without question, Toney takes great care throughout the book to praise those who could rise above the temptation of the moment. Such people could put aside the main chance, or the opportunity to "kick 'em when they're down." For example, Toney takes pains to distinguish the "colored soldier" guards in Maryland from their commander, a gentleman of honor. Similarly, Toney comments that several Northerners wanted to imprison Robert E. Lee right after the war. As the author describes it, Ulysses S. Grant responded to such threats by saying " '[i]t cannot be done so long as I am in command of the army.'" Likewise, Toney describes Lincoln's death as a tragedy for the South, because the president had understood the Confederacy's mistake and wanted the sections reunited again as one America.[22]

Of course, such imagery was standard Lost Cause and turn-of-the-century reunionist fare. This was the vocabulary of the cause of sectional reconciliation. From the example of the generosity practiced by the former soldiers, gray and blue, South and North would become truly one again. Or so it was hoped. And, as David Blight correctly observes, the fundamental significance of this reconciliation movement was that it created a reunion of whites and whiteness, thereby negating all the gains that African Americans had made out of the war and Reconstruction.[23]

So it may well be that Toney's *Privations* is simply

a memoir of sectional reconciliation through white rule. Yet, there is the suggestion of *something* beyond race and reunion.   In an era that seemed saturated with sordidness, opportunism, and the dark possibilities of pitiless social revolution, noteworthy examples of personal character, liberality, and self-restraint must have seemed refreshing.   Amidst the rampant Darwinism of the time, it must have been sobering to read of individuals who refused to grab everything by the throat.   Thus, even though Toney used his memoir to espouse the cause of white supremacy, it seems significant that he could not help but admire, and describe, those who could be charitable and magnanimous even in revolutionary times.

NOTES TO THE INTRODUCTION

1. Marcus B. Toney, *The Privations of a Private* (2d ed.: Nashville, TN.: Publishing House of the M. E. Church, South, 1907): [130], 122. (Page number from original edition provided in brackets.)

2. Will T. Hale and Dixon L. Merritt, *A History of Tennessee and Tennesseans: The Leaders and Representative Men in Commerce, Industry and Modern Activities* (Chicago and New York: Lewis Publishing, 1913), 5: 1507–509.

3. U.S. Census 1850, Population Schedules of the Seventh Census, Coffee and Davidson Counties in Tennessee, Microcopy 432, Roll 875, family entry number 1154.   U.S Census, 1850, Agricultural Census, Edgefield, Davidson County, Tennessee, entry number 30.   Quotation from Toney's entry in Colleen Morse Elliott, Louise Armstrong Moxley, eds., *The Tennessee Civil War Veterans' Questionnaires* (Easley, SC: Southern Historical Press, 1985), 5: 2066.

4. Elliott and Moxley, *Tennessee Veterans' Questionnaires*, 5: 2066.

5. Ibid.

6. For an extensive discussion of the hire-out system in antebellum Southern cities, see Midori Takagi, *"Rearing Wolves to Our Destruction": Slavery in Richmond, Virginia, 1782–1865* (Charlottesville: University Press of Virginia, 1999).

7. Hale and Merritt, *History of Tennessee*, 5: 1508.

8. King's Nashville City Directory, years from 1866–1920; copies at Tennessee State Library and Archives, Nashville.

9. Hale and Merritt, *History of Tennessee*, 5: 1508.

10. Biographical Sketch, *Confederate Veteran*, July 1896, 238.

11. On Cunningham see John A. Simpson, *S. A. Cunningham and the Confederate Heritage* (Athens: University of Georgia Press, 1994). Untitled column on Sally Claiborne Toney, *Confederate Veteran*, January 1893, 30; "Arbor Day at the Soldier's Home," *Confederate Veteran*, March 1910, 122.

12. Emphasis Watkins. Sam R. Watkins, *"Co. Aytch": A Side Show of the Big Show* (1882; reprint, New York: Macmillan, 1962; Collier Books, 1962), 17, 245.

13. Ibid., 244–45.

14. Toney, *Privations*, [13], 5.

15. Ibid., [88], 80.

16. Ibid., 130. Obit reference is to *Nashville Banner*, 1 November 1929, cited in Elliott and Moxley, *Tennessee Veterans' Questionnaires*, 5: 2067. Obit. reference refers to wife's name as Sallie.

17. Mrs. S. E. F. [Laura] Rose, "The Ku Klux Klan," pamphlet of a speech read to the 13th annual convention of the Mississippi division of the United Daughters of the Confederacy, 5 May 1909. There are no page numbers. Original copy in the Tennessee State Library and Archives.

18. Mrs. S. E. F. [Laura] Rose, *The Ku Klux Klan, or Invisible Empire* (New Orleans: privately printed, 1914), front dedication.

19. Toney, *Privations*, [125], 117.

20. The Tennessee legislature investigated Klan violence during the 1868 election year. See Military Committee, Tennessee

General Assembly, Senate, 1868, "Report of the Evidence Taken before the Military Committee in Relation to Outrages Committed by the Ku Klux Klan in Middle and West Tennessee," a pamphlet printed by the state printer, 1868. Copy in Tennessee State Library and Archives. See also Stephen V. Ash, *Middle Tennessee Society Transformed 1860–1870: War and Peace in the Upper South* (Baton Rouge: Louisiana State University Press, 1988); Peter Maslowski, "'Treason Must Be Made Odious': Military Occupation and Wartime Reconstruction in Nashville, Tennessee, 1862–1865," (Ph.D. diss., Ohio State University, 1972); Noel C. Fisher, *War at Every Door: Partisan Politics and Guerilla Violence in East Tennessee, 1860–1869* (Chapel Hill: University of North Carolina Press, 1997).

21. Toney, *Privations*, [115], 107.

22. Ibid., 84–88, 106, 116.

23. David W. Blight, *Race and Reunion: The Civil War in American Memory* (Cambridge: Belknap Press of Harvard University Press, 2001).

THE PRIVATIONS OF A PRIVATE.

CHAPTER I.

"The Girl I Left Behind Me."

THE purpose of this volume is to follow the life of
a Confederate private as I lived it and saw it lived by
others in the great struggle of 1861-65. The causes
leading to the Civil War are history, and need not be
enumerated here, except to say that our New England
cousins first engaged in the African slave trade, but,
finding their labor not profitable in that section, sold
their slaves to the Southern people, and a few years
afterwards looked upon the institution as horrible and
the Southern people as barbarians. Their continued
onslaught against it caused the separation of the Methodist Church, and we of the Southern branch have
been known as the Methodist Episcopal Church,
South. Many of the older people of that date pre-
dicted that the agitation of the question would lead
to the secession of the Southern states, which they
thought would be done peaceably. In their fight
against slavery in the South the abolitionists vilified
and abused the Southern people; their school primers
were illustrated with pictures of Southern farmers with
whip in hand chastising brutally the poor blacks. The
book written by Mrs. Harriet Beecher Stowe and the
drama therefrom, "Uncle Tom's Cabin," were a libel
upon the Southern people; yet they served their pur-

pose in inflaming the minds of the people North and prejudicing the South against the North. Mrs. Stowe may have visited a Southern plantation in which, the owner being absent, the overseer may have treated some of the slaves in a cruel manner; but this would have been an isolated case, and not representing the Southern people as a class. Mrs. Stowe could have said she had visited the Southern plantations and was surprised to see such a degree of harmony as existed between master and servant, maid and mistress, who were living as one great family in peace and harmony; that the master and servant had grown up boys together, that the young servant had attended his young master to school, and that they had played together the games common to young people of that day; and that the maid had attended the mistress from girlhood to womanhood, and there existed a mutual confidence between them; and there was the old black mammy who had nurtured the young master and mistress from her breasts, nursed them in her arms, and sang them to sleep many a night with her plaintive and sweet lullaby. Mrs. Stowe could have gone to black mammy's and Uncle Tom's cabin and said she was surprised with what neatness it was kept, and that the table was supplied from the products of the farm and old master's larder, and that the black folks dressed about as well as the whites, and that on Sunday Uncle Tom put on broadcloth and high silk hat and was better dressed than old master. After supper Mrs. Stowe could have seen Uncle Tom take down his banjo and play "Billy in the Low Grounds" and "Arkansas Traveler," while the young pickaninnies danced around him. Mrs. Stowe could have gone up to the mistress's room of the old plantation, and there have seen two old-fashioned wooden cradles, one on each side of the bed, the one containing the white the other the black baby; not that the blacks did not have time to attend to their offspring, but they would neglect them.

I will say here that my black mammy did not have the affection for her children that she displayed toward me. Next to my own mother, black mammy was as gentle to me; but with her own children I have seen her manifest an ungovernable temper, and twice in my boyhood I have seen my father take her children from her and say: "That child has been whipped enough!"

Mrs. Stowe could have visited our jails and penitentiaries and wondered why there were so few black prisoners; she could have been told that the blacks were imprisoned for murder and arson only, that for petty crimes the master was responsible and stood between the law and the slave; that they were not allowed to prowl after night without a pass from the master, or the patrol would get them; hence the slaves kept regular hours, which was beneficial to them.

Mrs. Stowe could have said that in some Southern states she found the whipping-post where, after being tied and their clothing stripped to the waist, the whites and blacks were given nine and thirty lashes for petty crimes. Of course this was severe punishment to both whites and blacks, but in those days it was not considered more cruel than prison walls.

Mrs. Stowe could next have visited the asylums for

the insane, and reported them full of whites, but she was struck with the absence of the blacks. The superintendent could have said to her: "Why should we have any slaves here? They have nothing to worry them, they are not troubled about finance or the business affairs of the world; old master supplies their every want, looks after all their families, clothes and feeds them, and furnishes his own physician in case of illness."

Surely Mrs. Stowe could have said: "In all my travels I have never seen a race happier or better satisfied with their lot—no thought of to-morrow, what they shall eat, drink, or wherewithal be clothed. Why should this condition of affairs be changed?"

Let us see. In 1860 I had two homes, both occupied by my negroes, one in what was then Edgefield, opposite Nashville, and the other near Lynchburg, Va. All my family except the blacks had crossed over the river, and I decided to move the Lynchburg family to Edgefield, Tenn., arriving during the heated campaign in 1860 which elected Mr. Lincoln President. Whether or not his election was a *casus belli,* I do not know, but I do know that the abolitionists of the North had so outraged the feelings of the Southern people that we felt we did not want any further affiliation with them. It is true that many of our old people who had been reared under the shadow of the Hermitage counseled against secession, and hoped that some compromise would be effected and the Union preserved; but the secession of South Carolina and the firing on Fort Sumter banished all their hopes, and war was inevitable, especially after President Lincoln called for 75,000 and then 300,000 troops to coerce the Southern states, as under our idea of state rights at that time each state should have been allowed to depart in peace; but such was not the case. The old Volunteer State was expected to do her duty, and the Governor's call met a hearty response, and the enlisting began in April, 1861. The young ladies were as enthusiastic as the young men; and if they found a fellow lukewarm, he was threatened with a petticoat and was not allowed to hang up his hat in their father's hall.

I thought Virginia was to be the theater of war for probably six or eight weeks. We would have a battle in which one Southern man would whip five Yankees with cornstalks, England would intervene, peace would be declared, and we should return home finding all our servants smiling at our home-coming. Vain thought! Four years and three months I was absent, and found no home on my return. The slaves were all free, but morally and financially in a much worse state than when I left them. Oh, if we could have had a Roosevelt across the water! But all the nations stood aloof and said, "Sick 'em, and may the heaviest guns and largest forces win!" There was too much revenue in war for some people to want it stopped.

I thought the first regiment enrolled would reach the seat of war early; and as the Rock City Guards, A, B, and C, were organized before the war, I enlisted in Company B, in which there were one hundred and four members, commanded by Captain James B. Craighead. We drilled in Edgefield and on the Square from April 15 to May 10, 1861, when we were mustered into the regiment, containing nearly one thousand men.

Our line extended across the Square. We elected as Colonel George Maney. We were sent for a few days to Camp Harris (named for Governor Isham G. Harris), on Elk River, near Estill Springs. While many of the young men of the South were adepts in the use of arms, we were novices as to cooking and washing. We knew that water and flour mixed made batter, and we knew that meat when fried made gravy; so with this much of the art acquired, we had fried dough, or what the boys called flapjacks. As to the washing—well, let that pass.

Instead of leaving Camp Harris for Virginia, we were returned to Camp Cheatham, where we were put through camp life and two daily drills. While here the young ladies from the Nashville Academy of Dr. Elliott presented us with a regimental flag by Miss Foster. Many cases of measles, and many fatal, took place at the camp, and the doleful dirge of the dead march often touched our hearts. We remained at Camp Cheatham nearly six weeks, all chafing under the delay and fearing the war would be over before we reached Virginia. We made one trip as a regiment to Goodlettsville, June 22, to vote Tennessee out of the Union. Soon thereafter we folded our tents and took the train for Nashville, where we stopped a few hours and bivouacked on the lawn in front of the Nashville Academy, where some three hundred young ladies of the city gave us a luncheon and assembled to say good-by.

I will say right here that nothing shall be written by me that will encourage young men to go to war. I would rather discourage, because nothing in it tends·

to elevate the young. Separate men from home influences and from the refining contact of female society, and they degenerate very rapidly. I don't suppose ten per cent. of the young men who go to war maintain their integrity. This is my opinion after careful study. I will say further that we left Nashville with as good a lot of boys as ever went to the front.

After luncheon we fell in and marched to the N. and C. depot to the tune of "The Girl I Left Behind Me." I was too young to be leaving a girl behind me; so I marched out with light step and joyous heart, not dreaming of the shock of battle, the roar of cannon, the hissing of bullets, and the groans of the wounded and dying. I looked to the right as we were passing the girls, and saw tears gathering in many eyes, for from the intuition of womanhood they knew that war meant death and destruction, and that many of the boys going to the front would fill soldiers' graves; and such was the case, for Company B lost seventy-one—only thirty-two reached home alive. It was only a short march to the N. and C. depot; in those days the N. and C. was spelled with small letters; now it is Nashville, Chattanooga, and St. Louis Railway. In those days we had small engines, after the pattern of the "General," with wood-burner furnace and big smokestack; we had ten box cars of 16,000 pounds capacity, and our speed was some fifteen miles an hour; now we have engines, as 251, 252, of nearly ninety tons, and developing a speed of sixty miles an hour with ten cars, including the coaches and Pullman sleepers.

In those days the N. and C. Railway track was on stringers instead of cross ties. The rails were laid on these stringers, and were flat like bar iron, and were nailed to the stringers, as they were too thin to use spikes. Sometimes the nails would draw out, and the end of a rail fly up, tearing up coaches. In those days the box cars were small, and 16,000 pounds was the maximum. Into these box cars we climbed and stood as thick as pins in a pincushion. When a fellow got tired of standing, he could climb to the top of the car, lie flat like a lizard, and hold on to the running board. About every fifteen miles we had to wood and water, and in order to rest themselves many of the boys would crawl down and spread out on the ground. In those days the passenger coaches were small, with little panes of glass; and in order to see out, one would have to raise the window. The N. and C. had one train from Atlanta to Nashville called the "owl train"—*out owl night*—left Nashville at 8 A.M., and arrived in Atlanta next morning at eight o'clock.

We reached Knoxville in two days, and much to our surprise went into camp just north of the railroad track and in quite thick woods. Knoxville was a small town in 1861, and had no houses north of the railroad. Now she has nearly a city north of the railroad, and she has crowded herself across the Tennessee River. It was while here that we heard that up in Parson Brownlow's home was a United States flag unfurled to the breeze, and some daring soldier said it should not flaunt, and went up to take it down; but Miss Brownlow, with pistol in hand, said: "The man that touches that flag will die!" Of course the Southern soldier did not die, as he had too much respect for the lady to disturb her flag. Miss Brownlow afterwards married my friend H. M. Aiken, and I had the pleasure of meeting her a few years ago, but said to her that I was not the soldier that went after the flag.

After a few days in Knoxville we boarded the train and went as far as Johnson City, where again we went into camp. Why those continuous delays I have never been able to find out, and my readers can imagine how we chafed under the delay, as the armies were gathering around Manassas for battle. We fussed and fumed for a few days, when the rush order came to run with all speed to Manassas. We sped the best we could; but when we reached Lynchburg, Va., the battle had been fought and won, many of the wounded had been brought to Lynchburg, and this was our first sight of the bloody war. The first wounded man I saw was Hon. H. A. Edmondson, of Roanoke, Va., who was a brother of John K. Edmondson, before the war sheriff of Davidson county, Tenn. Having nothing to do, we were held at Lynchburg, the City of Hills; and as we bivouacked near Black Water Creek on a steep hill, we had no use for a pillow, but if a soldier got crossways the hill he had a chance of rolling into the creek, far below.

While our troops had such success at Manassas, General Garnett had been killed at Rich Mountain, General Lee had been appointed to command the Department of West Virginia, and hitherward we were ordered; so we boarded the train for Millboro, Va., and stopped a few days at Staunton, where we met many of General Garnett's soldiers, and they were in a bad plight, many of them without shoes and with stone bruises on their heels. In a few days we were on the train for Millboro, where we disembarked after some eight hours' ride. Our destination was Cheat Mountain, some eighty miles from the railroad.

This was our first march fully equipped. Besides our gun, knapsack, haversack, and cartridge box, nearly all our boys had on one side a six-shooter Colt's

PRIVATE HENRY H. COOK.

revolver buckled around them, and on the other side was a large Damascus blade (made at a blacksmith's shop). This too had a scabbard and belt. The accompanying picture of Private Henry H. Cook, of Franklin, Tenn., will give my readers a full knowledge of the uniform and accouterments, as Henry (now Judge Cook) had it taken just before leaving home, and his

Company (D, Williamson Grays) was next to mine on the march. In Henry Cook's hand can be seen a small book. This is the pocket edition of the New Testament, which, when through with the picture, he placed in his knapsack. Each one of us was given a New Testament by our chaplain, Dr. Quintard, and on the fly leaf was written: "God is our sun and shield." We thought that "thrice armed is he who is armed with the word of truth."

From Millboro to Warm Springs, the first day's march, was fifteen miles, twelve of which were a gradual ascent. After we had trudged along some five miles in a sweltering August sun, I tried to give my six-shooter away, but could not find any one to accept it, and over in the bushes I threw it. I then unbuckled my Damascus blade, made an offer of that, but was likewise refused, and it was thrown into the bushes. I then tried to give away a blanket, but no one would accept, so away it went. I thought, probably, the war would end before the winter. By the time we reached the summit of the mountain nearly all the men in the regiment had disposed of their extra appendages by leaving them in the bushes. Looking down from the crest of the mountain, we could see in the valley, three miles distant, the hotels and cottages of Warm Springs. The descent to the springs was easy compared with the struggle up. Reaching the springs, we found a large bathing pool into which, from an iron pipe, the apparently cool water was gushing. Our men being thirsty, they crowded around the springs, and the first one to get a drink yelled out: "It is as hot as h—ll!" Of course the water was not cool, for it was one of the warm springs, known for its curative properties. Near by, however, was a spring so cold that one of the men said that it had ice in it. The next day we marched toward Valley Mountain, and in the evening heard immense cheering in our rear, the sound gradually coming toward the front; and looking around, we saw the cause. Sitting on "Traveler," clad in fatigue cap and jacket, and polished sword dangling from his side, with cap in hand as we gave a rousing cheer, rode General R. E. Lee, the pride of the Confederate army. At that time General Lee did not wear any chin whiskers; he had a large, dark mustache sprinkled with a little gray. He was the very picture of a magnificent general and horseman.

The third day from the Springs we pitched our tents near Valley Mountain, and then came the rain every day for some ten days, putting the roads in very bad condition. We were nearly sixty miles from the railroad, and a two-horse wagon could haul only some four barrels of flour, so with an army of about ten thousand men to feed it was a difficult problem. Our rations consisted of two small biscuits for breakfast and a like amount for supper. However, the country afforded some cattle as fine as I ever saw. They were very fat; and if we did not get enough bread and beef, we filled up on tallow. We had also some fine blackberries, which were as large as if they had been cultivated. One day I denied myself the usual two biscuits for breakfast, saved the dough, and had blackberry pies without any sugar for dinner.

We had not been in Valley Mountain very long till

one night after nine-o'clock taps the long roll sounded and we sprang to arms and took up our march toward Mingo Flats. The night was as black as Egyptian darkness. We crossed ravines and waded streams; and finally toward daylight, wet and weary, my regiment halted near an old stable. It would accommodate only a few, and the rest of us made a bed in the long dewy grass and got a few hours' sleep. The long roll seemed to be a false alarm, and after daylight we marched back to camp very tired and hungry, and without seeing a bluecoat.

One day I had been on picket duty near Mingo Flats, and on my return to camp in the evening I passed near General Lee's headquarters. There was a spring near by where I knelt to drink. General Lee hailed me: "Don't drink out of that spring; my horse uses it. Come and drink out of this spring near my tent." Out of deference to the General's request, I went up and drank of the spring; and as I passed him sitting on a camp stool I threw my hand to gun, palm extended, which is a private's salute to a general. General Lee returned it with the salute of the hand from the brow, which is a general's salute to a private. I mention this incident to show General Lee's regard for the private soldier. It made no difference to him whether a man wore the stripes of a private or the insignia of a major general: he had respect for the one and respect and consideration for the other.

Twenty miles from Valley Mountain was a road running from Beverly, Va., on the Baltimore and Ohio, to Staunton, crossing Cheat Mountain at a place on the mountain called Cheat Pass. It was General

Lee's object of this expedition to dislodge and destroy the enemy at this place. The fort at the pass was garrisoned by some three thousand men, while at Beverly they had some eight thousand men. Besides the fortifications on the mountain, the enemy had felled large trees outward from the fort and trimmed off the limbs and sharpened the many ends, so with a gun and knapsack and without an enemy in sight it would not be an easy matter to crawl through these obstructions to the fort. The plan of the attack was for General Rusk with his Arkansas brigade to cross Greenbrier River, which flowed near the base of the mountain, and assault the fort in front, while General Lee's troops should take it in the rear. September 12, 1861, at 9 A.M. was the hour, and the guns from General Rusk's brigade were to be the signal for our moving. We left Valley Mountain on the morning of September 10, with three days' (scant) rations. We marched on the valley road a while, and then commenced the ascent of Cheat Mountain. Our force for this expedition consisted of the First, Seventh, and Fourteenth Tennessee Regiments commanded respectively by Colonels Maney, Hatton, and Forbes, with General S. R. Anderson as brigadier. The other troops, commanded by Generals Donelson and Loring, moved down the valley road near the base of the mountain. My brigade was to get in the rear of the fortifications and cut off any reenforcements that might come. When we reached the crest of Cheat Mountain I saw the roughest and wildest country that I ever beheld, and we were to traverse it for twenty miles. The mountain was cut up into peaks and crags. Of course we had to march in sin gle file, and our brigade stretched out some three miles. General Lee and our commanders were in advance, and any command from them was passed back from the front man to the next in the rear, and so to the end of the line. We received and passed back many a time: "Keep quiet, keep well closed up." It was impossible to keep closed up; sometimes my leader would be thirty feet ahead of me, while I would be struggling over a huge bowlder or trying to crawl up the mountain by the aid of a sapling. The night of September 11 we bivouacked on top of the mountain only a few miles from the enemy's fortifications. It was about the roughest place I ever saw, and on account of the many rocks it was difficult to find a place for a spread. My comrade, George Keeling, was a delicate young man, and I carried his blanket, and after scraping off a lot of stones I spread George's blanket down, and we bunked together, covering with my blanket. Soon after we had retired it commenced to rain, and all night we had a continuous downpour. We not only got thoroughly wet, but our rations of biscuits washed into dough. Next morning I had a hard time carrying two wet blankets. We were in line early, and took up our march, and soon formed in line of battle on the Huttonville road, not far from the fortifications. In marching single file to the road, a bridle path crossed our line, and up this path, riding a magnificent horse, came a lieutenant of the Federal army. He appeared in a deep study, and came near riding into our line. We commanded "Halt"; and he looked up and said, "Did you men come from the clouds?" He was Lieutenant Merrill, of the Engineer

Corps. He was en route to the fort, but he was our prisoner. While we were in line on the road General Lee received a message from General Rusk saying: "Greenbrier River is at flood height; could not cross." We then received orders to return to camp, but before we moved the enemy fired into us from ambuscade, killing three and wounding eight of our regiment. We had no litters with us, and had to carry the wounded down the steep mountain side in blankets, four men to a blanket; and a new detail had to be made very often, as a man's fingers would cramp, and we would put the poor soldier down on the ground and change hands. On reaching the valley we had to carry the wounded some distance before we reached a farmhouse, and there we had to leave them and return to Valley Mountain, after falling in line several times on report that the enemy was following us. When we reached the camp at Valley Mountain we were in a bad plight, very hungry, and many of us barefoot. I was not quite barefoot, as I had one foot shod, the other bare. This campaign developed much measles and typhoid fever, and we filled the hotels at Warm Springs. Miss Jane Thomas and Miss Lavinia Taylor came out from Nashville to nurse the sick, and our boys ever remembered their kind ministrations.

General Rosecrans had commenced to invade Virginia via Charleston, and we received orders to meet his advance. On September 25, 1861, we took up our line of march for Big Sewell Mountain, some one hundred miles distant, and we made good mileage considering the downpour of rain we passed through. We reached Big Sewell Mountain September 30, and could plainly see the tents of General Rosecrans's army. On the night of October 3 we received orders to have our guns cleaned and in shape for the following morning; so we were up at half past three on the morning of October 4, and were ready to meet the enemy, as our information was that they were to attack us in the early morning; but we were disappointed. Upon looking over where the tents were the previous evening, we saw nothing of them. General Rosecrans had fallen back in the direction of Charleston. We started after him, but the road was in such a bad condition that we had to return to our camp in an old field on Big Sewell Mountain. We moved off the mountain October 11, and remained near by till October 22; we were then ordered to Huntersville, Va., where we remained till November 19, when we moved our camp on the Monterey road. As the weather was getting quite cold, it was decided to build winter quarters, and each mess vied with the others as to which could build the best cabin. But there were to be no winter quarters for us. Before the quarters were all completed we received orders to join General Stonewall Jackson at Winchester, Va., about two hundred and seventy-five miles distant; so on December 11 we took up our march at 10 A.M., and we moved to Gatewood, ten miles distant. We passed Warm Springs on the morning of the 13th, and on to Harrisonburg in a few days, and we were in the beautiful Shenandoah. On this march we had reveille before daylight, and soon after sunup we had eaten our breakfast, put a couple of biscuits in our haversack for dinner, and we would get into camp before sundown and soon have our supper. The First Tennessee Regiment had a splendid band, and as we marched through the beautiful towns of Bridgewater, Newmarket, etc., we would line up, get in step, and have "music by the band"; and the ladies would come out of the residences, lean on the front gates, and cheer us on our way. We reached the quaint old German town of Strasburg on Christmas Day; and if there was any whisky or eggnog left in that town, I did not know it. Between Strasburg and Winchester we saw many locomotives being hauled along the turnpike. General Jackson had captured them from the Baltimore and Ohio Railway at Martinsville. On December 26 we went into camp near Winchester on the Romney road.

CHAPTER II.

CAMPAIGN UNDER GENERAL STONEWALL JACKSON.

THE object of the expedition we were about to
make was to drive from Virginia General W. S. Hancock's forces, which had crossed the Potomac on pontoon at Sir John's Run and taken up their camp at
Berkeley Springs, not far from the Potomac. General Jackson's plan was to pass General Hancock's
right flank, get in his rear between the army and the
Potomac, and kill or capture as many as he could.
His plans were similar to the Chancellorsville movement, but we shall see that the weather knocked us out.
We struck tents at 8 A.M. Wednesday, January 1, 1862,
and the wind struck a good many of them, blowing
them down before we had a chance to draw the pegs.
It was a blustery day, but not very cold. We moved
eight miles to Pughtown, and bivouacked there. On
the morning of January 2 reveille sounded at five
o'clock, and before daylight we were on the move, but
made little headway, as the weather had turned in-
tensely cold, with a light snow. If a man was at the
head of the column he was all right; but after a few
companies had passed over, the snow became as slick
as ice, and skating would have been good if a fellow
had had skates. I bivouacked on three cedar rails and
built a rail fire on each side, and the red cedar popped
sparks on the cape of my overcoat, and when I woke
up I was afire.

Colonel Maney said that he thought we would get in the fight the next day. We were ordered to cook up all our rations. On the morning of the 4th we were formed in line and each man supplied with forty rounds of cartridges. We marched thirteen miles and reached a point three miles from Bath, or Berkeley Springs, and camped in the woods. It snowed heavily that night, and was extremely cold. There was little sleep for us. On the morning of the 5th we moved on Bath, and as we formed a line a short distance from the town, which was situated on a hill of considerable proportions, the enemy's battery opened fire upon us. General Stonewall Jackson rode upon Old Sorrel. The General wore a skull cap, a blouse, gray jacket, and the reins hung loosely on Old Sorrel's neck; he looked more like a plow horse than a war steed. With a twinkle in his eye General Jackson said to Colonel Maney: "Colonel Maney, I want the Virginians [alluding to his old regiment] to take that battery. They have had some rations since your men." We yelled out: "General, we do not want any rations; let us capture the battery." General Jackson replied: "Colonel Maney, move your regiment by companies to the right." We made a gallant charge, but when we reached the guns only two of the enemy were in sight. It was a feint to cover General Hancock's retreat across the Potomac on his pontoon, but he could have crossed on the ice, as it was nearly twelve inches thick.

While we moved to the capture of the battery Turner Ashby with his black horse cavalry charged into the town, capturing a few prisoners. It was an inspiring sight—the black horses of Ashby charging down the valley. We captured some rations, which we devoured in short order. The next day (Sunday) we moved six miles from Bath, and took up our position opposite Hancock, Md., a beautiful little town on the mountain side, and General Hancock had occupied the town; but alas! the Potomac River separated us, and it was filled with floating ice. The next day about 9 A.M. General Jackson sent a courier across the river. We watched the horse struggling through the floating ice, and cheered as it brought the rider safely to the other side. General Jackson's order was to move the noncombatants out of town, as he would commence to bombard at 12 A.M. At the hour named our batteries opened up a brisk fire, and General Hancock rushed some batteries behind the Methodist church and replied furiously. At intervals the dueling was kept up into the night, and it was a grand sight to see the solid shot moving as balls of fire. During a part of the cannonading in the daytime I stood near General Jackson and Colonel Robert Hatton, of the Seventh Tennessee. Both sat upon their horses as immovable as statues. It was said of General Jackson that he was a predestinarian. The Presbyterian boys might have explained the meaning of the term. It was also said that he was a fatalist. This was a term that I think would have been difficult for any of the boys to explain. I believe, however, that General Stonewall Jackson had that faith in God that lifted him above the field of battle, and, living or dying, he was the Lord's; then why should he be disturbed by the roar of cannon or the bursting of shells? That night a detail was to be made to picket the Potomac, with orders not to light any fires, because the enemy might fire at us from the opposite bank. Sergeant J. W. Carter, of Company B, commenced near the head of the roster for a detail, and many of the boys were sick. Captain Patterson said: "I cannot excuse any more; the sick must go to Dr. Buist and get an excuse." The roll call was continued, and I was a long way down the list; yet my name was reached, and I answered: "Am always on hand." Captain Patterson turned to Sergeant Carter and said: "How many roll calls has Toney missed since leaving Big Sewell Mountain?" He replied: "Seventeen." Captain Patterson said: "To-night's duty on picket wipes them all out." Gallant, chivalrous John S. Patterson, how I loved him! He was as gentle and modest as a woman. How my heart ached when I buried him the following October at Perryville, Ky.! In regard to the missing of roll call, I never regarded it as a dereliction of duty, therefore on the march from Sewell Mountain frequently when roll was called I was off foraging. In army parlance foraging was to send one of the mess out to buy something to eat, provided he had the money; if he did not have the money, he was to *take* the food. It was related of two comrades who lived near Murfreesboro, and who were sent out by their mess with one dollar to purchase supplies, that they returned with five cents' worth of bread and ninety-five cents' worth of whisky, and those that liked to imbibe complained of the purchase of so much bread. In regard to the roll call, it is a breach of duty to neglect when any service is to be performed, because it puts an extra and more frequent burden on your comrades. If I had used the army parlance term, and said "stood picket" that night, I should have missed it. I ran picket for four hours around and around a big tree; I had to do it to keep from freezing. I did not have anything to eat the previous day but some raw corn taken from artillery horses, and chewed the sprigs of sassafras bushes.

Captain F. S. Harris told me that he had traveled in that section much since the war, and that a citizen of Hancock, Md., had told him that on the two nights we were there the mercury was sixteen degrees below zero; and I do not doubt it. Many of our boys would get in that stupor which precedes death by freezing, and we would have to seize them roughly and keep them moving to prevent freezing. When relieved by another detail, about 3 A.M., I crawled in under an oilcloth and blanket and got a few hours' sleep. A fall of snow during the latter part of the night served to keep us warm. Looking from under the blankets next morning, we could see many of the boys sleeping beneath their snowy couches, which resembled graves. A detail of Company C was made to guard the medical stores of General Jackson, which were in wagons. The boys found in one of the wagons a cask of brandy. Getting hold of an auger, they notified the boys in camp to have some kettles ready. Going under the wagon, they bored through the body into the cask, and thus filled their vessels. General Jackson relieved them from duty, but did not punish them. I presume he thought they were excusable under the weather conditions. We were sorely disappointed in not being able to engage the enemy. It is true that we forced them across the river, but they could return in a few days after we left. General Jackson succeeded in destroying a dam in the Potomac River which fed the Chesapeake and Ohio Canal, and cut off canal communication between Cumberland, Md., and Washington, D. C.

On the morning of January 8 reveille sounded very early, and we moved slowly to Bath over a very slick, icy pike. The next morning there was another early reveille; and we made only seven miles that day, on account of the condition of the pike and blockade of wagons. On the 10th we were at Munger's Cross Roads, awaiting orders. Sunday, January 12, Dr. Quintard preached for us.

On my way to the post-office tent to mail a letter home General S. R. Anderson hailed me, and asked where I was going. I told him, whereupon he reached into his pocket and gave me a letter, saying earnestly: "I wish I could put myself into that letter and be sent home."

On the morning of January 13 we had early reveille, struck tents, and moved down to headquarters. Many of our boys were on the sick list, and when we went into Winchester we had only twenty-five able-bodied men left in Company B; and other companies were depleted in proportion. Out of my mess of ten only two of us were ready for duty, and we had the extra blankets of eight men. The town of Winchester was overrun with soldiers, and all the houses were filled to overflowing.

On January 14 we started to Romney, Va., which was situated on the bank of the beautiful south branch of the Potomac. On account of the ice and sleet we made only a few miles. On the 13th we crossed Capon River, and made only six miles during the day. The 16th of January we made only nine miles. and camped within eleven miles of Romney, which the enemy evacuated, leaving a lot of stores. On January 17 we were within four miles, and bivouacked with the regiments of Colonels Hatton and Forbes. Our cavalry occupied Romney, and we had nothing to do except to go into the town and get some rations. We were given a lot of provisions and drew quantities of butter, the first and only rations of butter I had seen issued during the war.

I went into Romney and took dinner at a private house on January 21. I met Major Yost, our quartermaster, and he said that he had heard that our brigade was going to Hanging Rock, some three miles from Romney, to winter quarters. Was the First Tennessee Regiment to go into winter quarters? We shall see.

Friday, January 24, we moved through Romney and reached Hanging Rock, and camped one-quarter of a mile from the Potomac. On January 25 Colonel Hatton's regiment moved down to Suspension Bridge, and camped near there. Some of our boys who went back to Winchester began coming into camp on January 26. They thought we would have a fight, and did not wish to miss it. On January 29 I crossed the south branch of the Potomac in a skiff, and saw the residence of Colonel Washington, who was on General Lee's staff, and who was killed in the Cheat Mountain campaign. Colonel Washington was the nearest living relative of General George Washington.

We got too near the enemy's pickets, and had to wait until nightfall to recross the river. At eleven o'clock at night our camp was aroused by the beating of the long roll, and we tumbled out of our tents in quick order. After the regiment was formed, my company was detailed to picket the ford. January 31 closed a very disagreeable week; it had snowed or hailed during the entire week.

On February 2 we had orders to be ready to move at a moment's notice, as the enemy were preparing to cut us off. On the 4th we moved from camp as rapidly as the weather and the wagons would permit. On February 5 we camped one mile from Capon Bridge, and on February 7 we reached our old camp at Winchester, which we left on January 1.

On February 8 I went into Winchester to get some clothing from Nashville brought by Lieutenant Van Leer. I learned that my package was lost at Manassas Junction. On February 9 we heard of the fall of Fort Henry, and this made us fear the loss of Fort Donelson. On the 14th of February my mess built a chimney to our tent, and we were prepared for the six-inch snow that fell on the 15th.

Colonel Maney had been to Richmond, and had the regiment detached from the Virginia army, and ordered returned to Tennessee to support Fort Donelson. The fatalities of the campaign were three soldiers frozen to death.

CHAPTER III.

THE RETURN TO TENNESSEE.

ON February 19 we left Winchester, arriving at Lynchburg on the 21st. We went into camp near that city, not knowing when we could proceed farther, on account of many washouts between Lynchburg and Bristol. Sunday, February 23, was a dark day for us, for we heard of the evacuation of Nashville. On February 27 I note from my diary: "Feel a great anxiety for the loved ones at home, but cannot get any message." On March 5 the railroad expected to resume traffic, but there were no trains moving. On the morning of March 6 we started for Bristol, the left wing of the regiment ahead of us. We reached Knoxville March 10, and remained there until the 12th, when Colonel Maney arrived and said that the right wing would proceed to Bridgeport, Ala., to guard the bridge there. We were held in Knoxville until Sunday, February 23, when we loaded baggage and proceeded to Chattanooga, where we went into camp one mile from the city. Fred Berry, of Company B, died February 21, at 6 P.M., and on the morning of February 22 Company B escorted his remains to the depot for forwarding to Nashville.

We had guard, drill duty, and dress parades daily at Chattanooga. On March 28 we heard of General Stonewall Jackson's victory at Kernstown. We left Chattanooga April 1 at 8 A.M., and arrived at Bridgeport at 11 A.M. and went into camp near the railroad bridge; in the meantime the left wing of the regiment went forward to Corinth. On April 4 we were ordered to cook three days' rations and to leave at 9 A.M. We boarded the train, and the order was countermanded and we disembarked and remained in camp till April 5, when ten box cars were backed up and we loaded at 7 A.M. These cars had been hauling bulk bacon, and they were very greasy. We slipped and slid, but could not slide very far, as we were packed in closely. We reached Stevenson at 8 A.M., and remained until 1:30 P.M., April 6, when the news reached us of the battle of Shiloh and the death of General Albert Sidney Johnston. We did not reach Corinth until Monday, April 7, at 10 A.M. We saw a large number of Federal prisoners, and the old Tishomingo Hotel was turned into a hospital and filled with our wounded. General Johnston's body had arrived, and was in a residence near by. On the morning of April 8 we were ordered to cook five days' rations, and on the morning of the 9th we left Corinth for the Shiloh battlefield. We met a large number of wagons and all kinds of conveyances carrying our wounded to Corinth. We marched over a dirt road, through swamps and water, reaching General Breckinridge at sundown, and slept in some vacant tents that were left by the enemy. Reveille sounded early on the morning of April 10, and we were soon under arms. We marched by General Breckinridge's headquarters, were drawn up in line of battle all day, and went back to our quarters in the evening. On Friday, April 11, it rained nearly all day, and we stayed in our tents until 5 P.M., when we were called out in the rain, but soon afterwards ordered back.

In camp all day April 12, and General Forrest's cavalry scouts said that there was no sign of the Federals south of where Shiloh was fought, but that they were under cover of the gunboats at Pittsburg Landing. We left Shiloh Sunday, April 13, on our way to Corinth, and after getting lost in the woods several times reached the camp at twelve o'clock Monday, April 14, where we found the left wing of the regiment, and listened to the boys, who gave us a graphic picture of the fight and regretted that we were not with them. We expected the next battle at Corinth, and for days and weeks worked on the fortifications and drank water the color of soapsuds. One had no trouble to get water at Corinth: all you had to do was to shovel out a few spadefuls of earth, and the hole would soon fill with water.

After completing out breastworks, we were expecting an attack daily by General Grant's forces, but were disappointed. Our pickets were very close together, and for days there was the rattle of musketry and hissing of bullets. The foliage was very thick, and frequently men would be shot from guns held by soldiers up in the trees. Often we had to crawl out to relieve the pickets. One of our men was shot as he poked his head around a tree.

On May 30 the enemy moved as if to flank us, and on May 31 we were en route to Tupelo, Miss. The Federal cavalry dashed around our army near Guntown and fired a train of ammunition, and the explosions could be heard for some distance. We reached

Tupelo June 10, and went into camp there. We had the regular routine drill twice a day and dress parade in the evening. We remained in Tupelo until July 20; and learning that the Federals were withdrawing their troops from Corinth toward Nashville, it was decided by our authorities to invade Kentucky.

CHAPTER IV.

Bragg's Invasion of Kentucky.

Our army was moved to Chattanooga, Tenn., by two routes: one by Selma, the other by Mobile. We went by train to Mobile, and there embarked on the side-wheel steamer *Dixie,* and were three days and nights reaching Montgomery, Ala., where we camped a few days, and then went by train to Atlanta, thence to Chattanooga. While we were on the Alabama River near Selma our boat landed for wood, and the boys spied a watermelon patch, and in a few moments the entire crop, green or ripe, had disappeared. In the meantime the owner boarded the boat, and Colonel Fields ordered every man to pay the farmer for the melons, and that he should be paid for either green or ripe; and the farmer got his pay. We remained for some days in Chattanooga, and on August 19 we were ferried across the Tennessee River on a steamboat, and took up our line of march across Walden's Ridge toward Pikeville and Sparta. When we reached Sparta, it was in ashes. Instead of proceeding to Nashville, we went to Gainesboro, where we crossed the Cumberland River, and were on the dark and bloody ground of Kentucky. While the march over Walden's Ridge and the Cumberland Mountains was a little fatiguing, they did not compare with Cheat and other Virginia mountains. Yet we were to encounter a march which was full of suffering, but of a variety which we were to experience for the first time. After we left Tomkinsville, Ky., we met a drought then prevailing in Kentucky. The dirt roads were very dusty, and sometimes we could not see ten feet ahead. The perspiration caused clots of mud to form in our eyebrows, hair, whiskers, and mustaches. At nightfall when we went into camp, very little water could be found, and frequently we drank out of the ponds in the barn lots. How many wiggletails and tadpoles I have drunk will never be known. When we reached Glasgow, Ky., General Buell was moving his army out of Nashville. There was a garrison (well fortified) of four thousand Federals at Woodsonville, a village of three or four houses opposite Munfordville, Ky. It was General Bragg's intention to capture this fort before General Buell could reach there. A short time previous to this, General Chalmers, of Mississippi, had stormed this fort and lost twelve hundred men. Our object was to get in the rear of these fortifications. We left Glasgow at sunrise with one day's rations, and marched rapidly in an easterly direction. We had some twelve thousand men and twenty-seven pieces of artillery. In marching along the road shaded by a lot of black-jack trees, we saw a countryman with a barrel of water on a sled drawn by a horse. We did not ask for a drink, but in a few moments the barrel was empty. The poor fellow said: "I have not a drop of water at home, and my wife and children are suffering." We felt sorry for him, but such is war.

We crossed Green River before midnight, and about 3 A.M. we were in Munfordville, and formed a line

of battle in the suburbs of the town. Company B was
in the cemetery, and I slept until sunup with a grave
for a pillow. Our artillery had been placed in position
not far from the Louisville and Nashville bridge, and
considerably higher than the Federal fort in Woodsonville. They saw that we were in a position to shell
them out, and at sunrise up went the white flag, and
we marched four thousand prisoners out and paroled
them. The advance of General Buell's army had
reached Bowling Green; and in a few days many of
his men reached our line without guns and surrendered, saying that they were tired of the war. After
the capture we expected General Bragg to do one of
two things: either move on General Buell at Cave
City, or go to Louisville. The authorities in Louisville
expected the latter, and every able-bodied man in
Louisville was called on to throw up fortifications; but
General Bragg did neither of the two things expected,
but he marched us eight miles toward Louisville and
went into camp at Bacon Creek. Next day he marched
us back to Munfordville, and then again to Bacon
Creek; and one night we camped at the side of the old
stage road near Bacon Creek, and it poured rain all
night. The little sleep I got was on three rails. From
Bacon Creek the army moved through Elizabethtown,
Hodgenville, New Haven, and went into camp at
Bardstown, Ky., twenty-seven miles from Louisville.
While here Governor Hawes was inaugurated Governor of the State. General Bragg issued a proclama-
tion calling on the Kentuckians to flock to his standard, and we fired a few volleys from the artillery, which
broke all the glass in the windows of the courthouse.

While we were in camp at Bardstown, General Buell's army marched to Louisville; and while we were playing soldier and living high in the blue grass country and losing men, General Buell was recruiting his army, and was soon ready for an advance; and we moved to Springfield, Perryville, Danville, and from Danville to Harrodsburg, and then back to Perryville —a forty-mile march to no purpose, for we did not need the exercise. On the night of October 7, 1862, we marched again through Harrodsburg and bivouacked after midnight in the suburbs of the little town of Perryville. When we formed in line and stacked guns for a few hours' rest, Company B was again in a cemetery. Was it a bad omen that twice recently our company slept in a cemetery?

Next morning Company B moved out of the cemetery to cook one day's rations. Seven of my mess dipped their hands in the same skillet. They were all stalwart men of brawny arm. That evening when the smoke of battle lifted, five of my comrades were dead, and the sixth wounded. Early in the morning we formed in line and moved slowly through the town on the Harrodsburg pike, which we left some half mile beyond Perryville, and turned to the left, crossing Chaplin Creek, or river, as it is called there. About three o'clock we were in line of battle on our extreme right and in a valley of the Chaplin River two and one-half miles from Perryville. There had been some skirmishing before our arrival, and about three o'clock the musketry and cannonading became quite brisk, the shells falling around us as we climbed the fence in battle line. We crossed Chaplin River, ascended a

high bluff, and when we reached the height Colonel
Savage's Sixteenth Regiment was hotly engaged with
the enemy. To uncover from Colonel Savage we had
to move by the right flank, and while executing this
move some of our men were wounded. When we
uncovered, we again moved by the left flank. General
Leonidas Polk rode up and asked: "What regiment
is this?" The answer was: "The First Tennessee."
He then said: "Capture that battery."

It was Parsons's eight-gun battery, supported by an
Ohio brigade (Germans) in command of General Jackson, of Hopkinsville, Ky. They would not stand the
charge, but ran in great disorder, leaving the battery
in our possession. In attempting to rally them General Jackson was killed, and his body fell in our line
of march. On a hill in the rear of where we captured the Parsons battery was Bush's Indiana battery,
supported by the First and Twenty-first Wisconsin
Regiments and another brigade of infantry. In
charging this battery we uncovered our left flank, and
were subjected to an enfilade fire from the enemy,
which played havoc with our men. We had ten men
killed in attempting to carry the colors. We lost some
two hundred and fifty men in a short time. Our boys
got so close to the battery that the smoke covered
them. Young Tom Lanier was killed some thirty feet
from the battery, not by the artillery, because we were
under the crest of the hill, and the pieces could not be
depressed so as to reach us, but the men supporting the
battery were the ones that caused most of our trouble.
Colonel Patterson was slightly wounded in the wrist,
but he tied a handkerchief around it and continued to

give orders until a grapeshot hit his mustache, going through his head, killing him instantly. Captain Pilcher was quartermaster, but he was in the thickest of the fray, receiving a wound that came near causing his death. Company B lost fourteen killed and thirteen wounded. Among the dead was a young man named Robert S. Hamilton. He came to Nashville in 1860, and was a proof reader in the Southern Methodist Publishing House. We were very intimate friends. He was an ardent secessionist, while his family in Kentucky were divided on the war question. In the charge Robert was shot through the forehead, and fell not far from where Tom Lanier and gallant Jack Goodbar fell. Colonel Fields detailed me to stay and take care of the wounded and do the best I could to bury the dead. After getting all the wounded off, with the aid of reflected rays from a burning barn which the exploding shells fired, I penned the following:

BATTLEFIELD, PERRYVILLE, KY., October 8, 1862.

Mrs. W. C. Hamilton, Lexington, Ky.: Robert was killed in gallant charge this evening. Will take care of remains until you arrive. MARCUS B. TONEY.

Mrs. Hamilton was Robert's sister-in-law, and I wrote to her because his brother, W. C. Hamilton, was a Union man, and Robert never wrote a line to him; but all his correspondence was with his sister-in-law, and he always read her letters to me; therefore I wrote to the sister-in-law rather than to the brother. The blue and the gray mingled together all that night removing the wounded. I approached one of the blue and asked him if he would deliver the note to Mrs. Hamilton, and he promised me that he would.

It was a sad sight that night as I gazed upon the upturned, ghastly faces of our dead; and the cries of the wounded for "water!" "water!" "water!" were heartrending. Before daylight all of our wounded had been brought from the field. A farmer named Goodnight, who lived some half mile from the battlefield, had deserted his house on the eve of battle, and we turned it into a hospital. On the second floor in the small room were the following: J. H. Woldridge, B. P. Steele, T. H. Maney, M. B. Pilcher, Mac Campbell, Lute Irwin, J. H. Wheless, and Lieutenant Hammond. These eight men were my patients. Four of them were on the bedsteads and four on the floor. Comrade Woldridge lost both of his eyes, and Captain Pilcher, Captain Steele, Lieutenant Maney, Mac Campbell, and Lute Irwin were all badly wounded. For three nights I did not close my eyes in sleep.

About the third day after the battle a messenger came upstairs and said that a lady was in waiting to see me. This was my first meeting with Mrs. Hamilton. Mr. Hamilton was with her, and they brought a hearse and casket, and a carryall with blankets and provisions for our wounded. I accompanied Mr. and Mrs. Hamilton to the battlefield. I had buried twenty-seven of the Rock City Guards in a gully near by where they fell, and not far from the battery that they charged so gallantly. I did not have any implement to bury with, but with the use of a breastplate taken from the body of a dead Federal I invented a tool which formed a kind of scoop, and with this covered our boys with the dirt. I had buried Robert Hamilton at the head of the twenty-seven, and when we reached the spot I raked the dirt from his face and said: "Mrs. Hamilton, this is Robert." "Is it possible," she replied, "that these are Robert's remains?" I said: "I will soon satisfy you." Reaching down, I caught one of his hands, and, brushing the dirt away, I said to her: "Do you see this?" She replied: "I am satisfied." Robert was a very studious young man, and in his deep studies I have seen him bite his nails to the quick, and frequently brought blood. When Mrs. Hamilton saw the hand and the condition of the finger nails, she knew they were Robert's. When the body was taken to the hospital and prepared for burial, there was no doubt in her mind. We expected to bury W. J. Whitthorne, of the Maury Grays, Columbia, Tenn., but the body could not be found. He was shot through the neck, and Dr. Buist said that he would not live until we got him to the hospital. Billy Whitthorne, as we all called him, is living this year (1907). He raised a company at Columbia during the Spanish-American War, and went to the Philippines. He was elected major in the regular army, and later lieutenant colonel of the First Tennessee National Guards, and I am a private in Company B, Confederate Veterans, of the Guards. We had a similar case in John Sullivan, the gallant Irishman of the Martin Guards. His wife accompanied him to the war, and was very valuable in assisting the boys in needlework and cooking. Sullivan had a hole in his forehead that exposed a part of the brain. Mrs. Sullivan was at the hospital when the fight was going on, and when we reported after midnight that John was left on the field for dead she said that she would go out and look after him. She was a stalwart woman, and brought John on her shoulder to the hospital. About two weeks after that Dr. Buist bought a carryall, placed Captain Woldridge, Mr. and Mrs. Sullivan in it, and started them through the country to Pulaski. Near Lebanon, Ky., they were captured and sent to prison.

A few weeks after the battle Captain Steele was removed to Harrodsburg, and Mrs. C. H. Rochester came after Captain Pilcher, T. H. Maney, S. B. Shearon, and myself, and we were taken to her residence, near Danville, Ky., where we were royally entertained. Colonel Rochester and the elder sons were in the Confederate army, leaving Mrs. Rochester and the young ladies and boys at home. The families of Captain Merritt S. Pilcher, George S. Kinney, and Henry C. Hensley had refugeed from Nashville to Louisville.

Dr. Buist sent a message to Captain M. S. Pilcher saying that if Matt were sent to prison he could not possibly survive. Captain Merritt Pilcher had a stanch friend in Louisville, Mr. John B. Smith, who stood very close to General Jere Boyle, commanding that district, and through his influence we received the following:

HEADQUARTERS DEPARTMENT OF KENTUCKY,
LOUISVILLE, October 13, 1862.

The bearers hereof, Capt. Matthew B. Pilcher and Private Marcus B. Toney, will be allowed to report at these headquarters without a guard so soon as the wound of Captain Pilcher's will permit.　　　　JERE BOYLE, *General.*

We remained at Mrs. Rochester's nearly four months, and almost despaired of getting Captain Pilcher to Louisville. In addition to his great suffering from the wound, a spell of pneumonia gave him a

setback. Soon after convalescing he came near
bleeding to death, and I mounted a horse and went
rapidly to Harrodsburg for Dr. Buist. Finally he
recovered so far as to allow us to proceed, and he
desired to go via Lexington to visit for a few days his
relatives, Mr. Hiram Shaw and family; so we proceeded to Nicholasville by stage, and thence to Lexington by rail. Mr. Shaw was a stanch Union man, and
was a dealer in gents' furnishing goods. A few weeks
before we reached there, General Morgan's men raided
his store, exchanging their old headgear for his fine
hats, and some of the boys wore off his best tiles;
therefore I felt a hesitancy in going to the Shaw
domicile. But we were treated in a most generous
manner. A few nights after reaching there, we paid
a visit to another family of the Shaws, where there
were three young ladies. General J. Q. A. Gilmore
was a visitor, and he asked one of the ladies who
we were. She informed him, and the next day we
received orders to report to General Gilmore's headquarters. Accordingly we did so, and he said in a
very brusque manner: "I wish to know by whose authority you Rebels are free." I replied, "By authority
of General Jere Boyle, of Louisville"; and I placed our
parole in his hands. He glanced over it, and said:
"This is not General Boyle's district; I am commanding here, and my name is General J. Q. A. Gilmore.
You will get ready to go to Louisville with a guard
this evening. Report here at three o'clock." I said:
"All right, General Gilmore. Your order will be
obeyed, but we were ignorant of the infringement on
your territory." At 3 P.M. we were there, and so was

the guard with his gun. We wired Captain Pilcher that we would be in about 8 P.M., under guard. When we reached Frankfort, we found that the railroad bridge had been burned, and we had to cross on the ferry. In going through the city many ladies turned out and escorted us to the ferry. When we reached Louisville, Captain Meritt S. Pilcher was pacing up and down the platform, and appeared more disturbed than we were. After greeting us, he said: "Boys, I have been trying all day to see General Boyle; but one of his children has smallpox, and he is at home. The officer of the day says he cannot release you, and you will have to go to prison at Tenth and Broadway." We could do nothing but obey. When we reached the pen we found there four hundred prisoners who had been captured at Fort Donelson. It was quite a filthy place, without sleeping accommodations. We had some salt pork, stale bread, and coffee without sugar. As we had been living for four months on the fat of the blue grass region, we could not eat the prison diet, and were glad to hear our names called at the wicket about nine o'clock next morning, where we signed parole to the National Hotel; and when we reached the sidewalk we found Captain Pilcher and Mr. John B. Smith with a carriage, and they escorted us to the hotel. We remained at the hotel for six weeks, waiting for the flag-of-truce boat for exchange. After the first week's confinement at the hotel, General Boyle extended our parole so as to allow us to attend church on Sunday, and we first went to Sunday school and then went to services at 11 A.M. Sometimes we went to hear the big gun of the Baptist Church, Dr. Lorimer, and then to hear Dr. Craik, of the Episcopal Church, and at 3 P.M. we attended vespers at the Cathedral, and at night church again. One Sunday morning in Dr. Lorimer's church Captain Pilcher was asked to teach the Bible class, and in the class were some of the boys in blue. The Southern people in Louisville treated us with much consideration and kindness, and the people who differed with us on the war issue treated us with respect. In the churches and on the streets we were frequently detained for hand shakes. We wore Confederate uniforms, but General Boyle requested that the brass buttons be covered. The Southern ladies visited us frequently at the hotel, and we returned many of the visits at their residences on Sunday. I recall these names among those who were exceedingly kind to us: Miss Fanny Jack, Miss Kate Quarrier, Miss Mary Miller, Miss Anna Caldwell, Miss Nina Smith (who after the war married Mr. H. Victor Newcomb, and later Mr. Ten Broeck). Captain Pilcher and myself did not indulge in wine, so we were much amused to receive from Miss Fanny Jack a bottle of wine with this toast: "Believe that in every drop of wine contained in this bottle is *mingled* a heartfelt prayer for the *ultimate* success of the Southern Confederacy." Evidently it was the toast which Miss Fanny wished us to enjoy rather than the wine. So the time drew near when we were to journey to Fortress Monroe for exchange at City Point, and Mr. John B. Smith called on General Boyle for an order to proceed without a guard. General Boyle said that he could favor us only as far as Cincinnati, and gave us the following:

HEADQUARTERS DEPARTMENT OF KENTUCKY,
LOUISVILLE, April 9, 1863.

General Ambrose E. Burnside, Cincinnati, Ohio: Capt. M. B. Pilcher and Private M. B. Toney have been on parole from these headquarters since the battle of Perryville, and have faithfully kept it. I will therefore be obliged if you will allow them to proceed to Fortress Monroe without a guard.   JERE BOYLE,
General Commanding Department of Kentucky.

Armed with this document and escorted by a large number of friends, we proceeded to board the steamer *General Lytle*. One of the ladies had purchased for me a large silk handkerchief. It was plain on one side, but on the other was the bonnie blue flag, and as the *General Lytle* steamed out from the levee Captain Pilcher and I were on the hurricane roof, and I unfurled my banner to the breeze, and received the cheers from the assembled multitude on the levee. We stopped at the Burnett House. Next morning at breakfast I said to Captain Pilcher: "There is General Burnside." He was sitting two tables from us. General Burnside at that time was trying Mr. Vallandigham for treason, and banished him through our lines at Shelbyville. I agreed with Captain Pilcher not to report as yet to General Burnside, because there were some friends in Covington whom we wished to meet, and did meet in our room at the hotel; and they got into such a boisterous discussion that one of them said: "Hush, boys; walls have ears." When we reported to General Burnside with General Boyle's letter, I noticed his brows contract, and he looked at us fiercely and said in a very abrupt manner: "This is a very peculiar request from General Boyle, and one entirely contrary to

War Department orders. *I cannot grant it.*" I replied: "Very well, General; do with us as you will, as we are subject to your orders." He thought a while and said: "I will do this: place you in charge of a lieutenant with his side arms. That will be better than going with a soldier and gun over you. Report here at six o'clock to take the train for Baltimore." We reported at six o'clock, and met the lieutenant, whom we found to be a nice gentleman and very companionable. We arrived in Baltimore and registered at the Barnum Hotel. After supper we retired early.

The next morning the lieutenant, after a visit to the provost marshal's office, said that the flag-of-truce boat would not sail for several days, and that they had smallpox very bad there. He said that we would remain in Baltimore. After breakfast he said: "Boys, I am going to see the city. I know you do not wish to go with me, and I don't care to stay with you. If you are arrested, tell them to wait till I come with the papers." Captain Pilcher and I had a letter to Noah Walker, wholesale clothier, and we started to his store, but had gone only two squares when we were arrested as spies. We told the detective that we were under orders for exchange, and under the control of a lieutenant of the United States Army, and if he did not believe our story he could accompany us to the hotel, which he did, and waited several hours. When our lieutenant returned he was very angry, and cursed and abused the detective severely. Next morning I said: "Lieutenant, we want to call at Noah Walker's. We wish you would go with us to the door, where you can leave us and resume your sight-seeing."

So he did. We presented our letter to Mr. Walker, and had a pleasant chat with him. He inquired especially after his friends in Louisville. When we arose to take our leave, he said: "Boys, wait a while. Come this way." We followed him up four flights of stairs. Coming to the fifth story, he unlocked a door and we entered another narrow flight of stairs; he locked the door on the inside, and put the key in his pocket. When we reached the head of the stairs, we found a large stock of Confederate uniforms. He said: "Mum is the word. I am running the blockade with these; and if it were known by the Federal authorities, my entire stock would be confiscated." We told him that our lips would be sealed. He said: "I did not bring you up here for a display, but I want each of you boys to select an overcoat." We did so, and he sent them to the hotel. The next morning we took passage on the Bay Line steamer for Fortress Monroe. Just after leaving Baltimore I saw a commotion in the ladies' cabin, and heard the word "Rebel" uttered excitedly. Presently the captain came to us and said: "Boys, I have an old lady aboard who is a regular virago. She says that she does not want to travel on the same boat with Rebels. I told her that you had paid first-class fare and were entitled to cabin-fare passage, but that doesn't quiet her. She is creating a terrible furor with the passengers. I wish you would go down on the deck. I will send your supper to you, the best we have on the table, and after supper I will bring you up to your stateroom."

The captain was a Baltimorean and a Southern sympathizer, and to accommodate him we went below till after the old lady retired, when we turned in to dream of the flag of truce. I hope the old lady has reached that land where there are no Rebels to molest or make her afraid.

When we awoke next morning, we were landed near the truce boat. The lieutenant took a receipt for us from the exchange officer, and bade us good-by as if he were sad in leaving us. I am sure we were sorry to give him up, as he was exceedingly kind to us. I wish that I had kept his name. We asked to be remembered to General Burnside for sending such a clever officer with us. Soon after boarding the truce boat we were sailing up the historic James River. The next morning we landed at City Point, where a like number of Federals were to be exchanged for us. Many cases of smallpox were on the lower deck of our truce boat, and it was difficult to get help to unload. Finally the captain said that if they were not removed he would take them back, so I volunteered to carry the patients off.

The exchange officer said that he would have to separate the officers and privates and send us to our commands in that manner. He was rather brusque in his order, which irritated us. Captain Pilcher said: "We have been in the hands of the enemy for six months. They not only would not allow us to be separated, but treated us in a more respectful manner than you have." This appeared to put a quietus on the officer, and he allowed us to proceed together, which we did as far as Knoxville, when we separated on account of the following accident. About fifteen miles west of Bristol, at three o'clock in the morning,

Captain Pilcher and I, with a lot of soldiers, were in the rear car, when a brake beam broke and fell in front of our trucks, throwing our car from the track and dragging it until it reached a sharp curve, when the coupling pin broke and we turned over several times, landing near the edge of the Watauga River. Captain Pilcher said that the first voice that he heard from the groans of the wounded was my query: "Captain, are you hurt?" He replied: "Yes; take these wounded men off of me."

As soon as we went over the lamps were smashed and it was very dark; but with the assistance of a comrade who had only a few bruises like mine, we succeeded in getting Captain Pilcher out through the end window. His arm was broken, but on arrival at Knoxville he said that he thought he would be able to travel in a week. As I had been absent for six months, I was anxious to get back.

CHAPTER V.

THE CHICKAMAUGA CAMPAIGN.

I FOUND the regiment on Duck River in the suburbs of Shelbyville. I was glad to be with the boys again. I did not rest long, for the regiment was busy making detail for digging fortifications, and I worked with pick and shovel.

The two great evils attending war are drinking and gambling. In 1863 the drink habit was much lessened in our army because the drinks were scarce and hard to get. Mr. McGrew kept a drug store on the Square in Shelbyville, and by some means it was ascertained that he had some whisky in the cellar, and one night some soldiers got into it and took the whole stock, consisting of about half a barrel; and the old mill, situated on the river, was frequently robbed of its stock; and in unloading commissaries at the depot the soldiers would make *mistakes* and throw meat under the depot, and at nightfall bring it to camp. The mania for gambling continued unabated. I have seen men gamble all night, and do a good deal of nodding on duty the next day. If they did not have money to gamble with, chips for fun would not be much amusement. I have seen on the march, just previous to an engagement, bits of pasteboard (decks of cards) scattered along so that the line of march could almost be designated by the scraps, and also by letters torn and scattered, because a soldier did not wish to be found dead on the field of battle with a deck of cards in his pocket, or prying eyes to read his letters from home; but I have never yet seen a soldier discard the little pocket Testament that his mother gave him when she sent him forth with her prayers.

Shelbyville was a place that could easily be flanked,

THE GAMBLING MANIA.

and Rosecrans was preparing for it. General Bragg hoped to give him battle on better vantage ground (for us), and selected Tullahoma, and we prepared to retire to that point in good order if General Rosecrans would permit. Our army commenced to retire—the infantry in front, General Wheeler's cavalry in the rear. Early in the morning I was on detail to proceed to the Nashville and Chattanooga depot and load up the commissaries. We worked with a will, and thought that we could get everything in the cars, but some of the detail early in the day found a lot of whisky and commenced to get drunk. About 3 P.M. we heard a tremendous boom, boom of our artillery on the Square, followed by a fusillade of musketry. The Federal cavalry had approached from the front and flank. Lieutenant J. R. McDaniel's (or Wiggins's) battery made a gallant resistance, and succeeded in getting his pieces away with the loss of only two. He lost a number of his men, however, the enemy riding into their midst and cutting them with sabers. In attempting to cross the Duck River bridge General Wheeler found it blockaded and swam his horse above it, having the belt of his sword shot away. As soon as I saw the stampede on the Square I ran into the depot, got some clothing and shoes out of a box there, and went down under the depot (which had open sides) and bivouacked in the dust with hogs and fleas, which were very industrious. After leaving the Square the Federal cavalry rode rapidly toward the depot. One of my detail, seeing them coming, staggered out near the Barksdale House and said that he could whip the whole Yankee army. It was only a short while before he was in Nashville, and later in Fort Delaware. I remained with my companions (hogs and fleas, and the dust made a pretty soft bed) till late in the night, and then by the aid of the stars kept in the direction of Tullahoma, where I found the First Tennessee next dáy in a beautiful black-jack grove about one mile north of the town. In front of the grove an avenue some two hundred feet wide by one mile long had been cut out, and it was a splendid place to fight in the open; but the enemy chose not to fight there. General Rosecrans's scouts came within three miles of us, our cavalry interposed, and General Starnes was mortally wounded. After a few days' rest we commenced to retire toward Chattanooga, and it was a rough march over the mountains, but nothing in comparison with Cheat Mountain. Soon after reaching Chattanooga we were put to work building two immense forts—one near where the Stanton House is now, and the other near the city cemetery, in the eastern suburbs of the city. The only service that the forts rendered was to conceal in the dirt bacon stolen from the cars, and hid there until a favorable time to remove it to the camp.

We had been in Chattanooga but a short time when General Rosecrans occupied Walden's Ridge and Raccoon Mountain. About the 15th of August our army moved out of Chattanooga. I did not know where we were going. In fact, it is not the business of a private soldier to know anything except to obey orders. I did not like to leave the forts, upon which we had expended so much labor, knowing that in a short while the enemy would be enjoying the fruits of our labor. We moved down the valley via Rossville, McLemore's Cove, and next day reached Lafayette, Ga., where we camped; the following day we faced again toward Chattanooga, and early next morning crossed Chickamauga River at Lee and Gordon's Mill, and were soon drawn up in battle array, when General Maney stood up in his stirrups and made a speech to the Tennessee boys, saying: "We shall soon

have an opportunity of striking again for our homes
and firesides, and to acquit ourselves like men worthy
of the old Volunteer State." Soon the firing of pickets
gave notice that the battle of Chickamauga was about
to begin. As the First Tennessee Regiment moved in
line through a thick wood of oak and pine, we struck
the enemy, who were posted on a hill much higher than
our position. General Cheatham rode in advance of
the line with hat in hand, and said: "Come on, boys."
The First Tennessee charged gallantly amidst a terrible cannonade. A shell exploded in front of us,
a piece striking the shoulder of Lieutenant W. H.
Webster, of the Maury Grays, from which he soon bled
to death. The enemy's infantry retired before our
charge, and we reached the crest of a ridge and were
ordered to "lie down." While in this position Ensign
Joe Campbell raised up on his arm, and a shot from the
enemy pierced his brain, and he was instantly killed.
The next day we were moved to the right of our
army and held in reserve nearly the entire day,
and late in the evening participated in the final
charge over the enemy's breastworks of black-jack
logs, and Chickamauga was ours, and the enemy
on retreat to Chattanooga, ten miles distant. General
Bragg has been much criticised because he did not
capture General Rosecrans's army before it was safely ensconced in the forts upon which we had expended so much labor. If General Bragg had had a
sufficient force of fresh cavalry, the feat might have
been accomplished; but it must be borne in mind that
we had been on the move some five days and nights,
with little sleep and short rations, and when the final

charge came, about dusk of September 20, our men fell down with the dead and wounded of the enemy inside of their former breastworks, and went to sleep. The next day we moved leisurely up to the crest of Missionary Ridge, and we lost comrade Eugene Topp, of Pulaski, who was shot by the enemy's pickets as we ascended the ridge. From Missionary Ridge we could see the enemy scattered around Chattanooga, and occupying our former forts. We moved down from the ridge and went into camp at the base, facing toward Chattanooga. We also occupied Lookout Mountain, and had one piece of artillery on the Point; but we could not throw a shell to the Nashville and Chattanooga depot, which was about three miles distant on an air line. Soon afterwards General Grant succeeded General Rosecrans, and he had a lot of guns casemated at Moccasin Point. We could look down on his batteries, but we could not depress our pieces so as to give him any trouble. A party of us would gather at the Point to attract his fire, and as soon as we would see the smoke, down we would fall, and the shell would whiz over us. Our pickets were on the bench of the mountain below the Craven House, and extended up Lookout Creek. A shell from Moccasin Point killed and wounded five of our men at one time. I was on picket duty one day on Lookout Creek, a Federal on the other side. You could take a run and jump across. I asked him how rations were. He replied that they were living on ox-tail soup. He said that Joe Wheeler had burned a number of bridges on the Nashville and Chattanooga Railroad between Nashville and Chattanooga, and that General Grant had started a train of some two hundred wagons with commissary stores, and when they reached Sequatchie Valley Joe Wheeler again appeared on the scene and burned the entire train ; the army was therefore greatly reduced in supplies.

In 1863 Chattanooga was not much of a town ; Market was the principal street, and that was filled with a lot of insignificant shanties, hence General Grant's army camped over the hills upon which beautiful residences are now located. His tents extended from the fort near the Stanton House to the river, while General Hooker's tents covered Raccoon Mountain. From the top of Lookout Mountain it was a grand scene at night—the bright camp fires of this large army ; and at nine o'clock the many bugles would blow taps, after the music from many bands had floated upward. On the night of November 24, 1863, we moved off of Lookout Mountain and took our position on Missionary Ridge. Part of the First Tennessee Regiment line was directly over the tunnel. From this position we could clearly see the entire line of General Grant's army moving out of Chattanooga in order of battle, extending nearly to Rossville. Just below where the Cincinnati Southern bridge is now located could be seen General Sherman's army crossing on steamboats, and it did not take him a great while to get a battery on one bench of Missionary Ridge, which was separated from our ridge by Chickamauga River and the Western and Atlantic Railway. I think his position was some higher than ours, and his battery annoyed us without doing much damage. General Grant's lines were drawing nearer and nearer to us, and our batteries were belching forth, and we could now and then see his men scatter from an exploding shell. Nearer and nearer they came until we could see the glittering steel and the flash of the officers' swords in the sunlight; nearer and nearer they came until lost to sight at the base of Missionary Ridge. We then took our position on the crest of the ridge, lying down and waiting for them to come in sight. We did not have a great while to wait. Soon we saw the long line of bluecoats advancing. We were hugging the ridge so closely that nothing but our heads peered over; so it was not so easy to see us, as the bushes were quite thick and many large trees were on the ridge. When the bluecoats got within a hundred feet of us the firing commenced, and they continued to advance, when Colonel Fields said: "Fire, boys, and charge." Down the ridge we went, the enemy keeping ahead of us. We got so close to them that Colonel Fields hit a Federal on the head with a rock, and comrade John Branch grabbed at the colors, tearing out a piece, but the sergeant got away with them. We followed them to the base of the ridge, where the town of Sherman Heights is now located. Finding them in the trenches which we had once made, we returned to the top of the ridge. It was now dusk, and we were still in line of battle and drawing some rations, when the order came to get away as quietly and quickly as possible. General Grant had pierced our center, and all were in danger of capture. We were the worst disappointed soldiers in the army. We thought our whole line as far as Rossville had made the same movement that we had, and would next move on General Grant and capture his army before it could get to our forts in Chattanooga.

Well, we did not stand upon the order of our going, but went out as rapidly as possible, every fellow taking care of himself. We went down many ridges and crossed the Chickamauga River on the Western and Atlantic Railroad bridge, and afterwards burned it. The next day we came to Chickamauga Station. There was a large pile of bacon there ready to be burned rather than to have it fall into the hands of the enemy. I fixed my bayonet and selected a small side of bacon through which I ran the bayonet, and was marching along thinking what a nice fry I would have for supper, when the enemy's guns opened on us, and the skirmish known as Cat Creek took place. I had to unfix my bayonet in order to load my gun, and the bacon was lost. Samuel Seay was wounded in this skirmish, and he begged the boys not to leave him in the hands of the enemy. We told him we would not, unless they got us; so four of us shouldered him, and we would now and then call for relief. We marched till late in the night before reaching Ringgold; and although Sam Seay was a light man, he got heavier and heavier. At one place where we crossed the Chickamauga River I got very wet, and it was a cold night—November 26. I rolled up my trousers as high as I could, and four of us started across with Sam, and I got into a hole up to my waist. Finally we reached a clump of black-jacks near Ringgold, through which ran a country road well filled with autumn leaves, and here we made our bed. We were sleeping soundly at sunrise when General Walker came riding swiftly, saying: "Get up, men; the Yankees will soon be here, and they will cut your throats." We moved out promptly, and as we had been the rear guard the day previous, we were now in the advance. We had just reached the narrow place where the stream is spanned by the railroad bridge, when the battle of Ringgold was fought; but we continued our retrograde movement until Dalton was reached, and, after camping there for some days and the weather getting cold, we built winter quarters south of Dalton.

CHAPTER VI.

CARRY ME BACK TO OLD VIRGINIA.

WHILE in winter quarters at Dalton, I received a letter from a relative saying that she would soon get married, and had woven on her loom a nice suit of jeans, and that I must come a week before in order that the tailor could make them. Therefore, I made application for a furlough, and it is not necessary to say here that I obtained a genuine one. My destination was New Canton, Va., on the James River, sixty-six miles above Richmond. I went via Columbia, S. C., and reached there without any money. As I had not drawn any clothing from the Confederate States Army for a year, I was entitled to so much money in lieu thereof. I think the paymaster paid me ninety-five dollars.

When I reached Petersburg I heard that the canal was frozen over between Richmond and New Canton. I therefore went from Petersburg to Farmville by rail, and thence horseback to New Canton, hiring a negro boy to bring the horses back. Near Buckingham Courthouse we had to ford Slate River. Some men were working in the low ground, and I asked them where to ford, as the river was much swollen. They pointed to a place above, and in my horse went; down the stream he swam, and I clinging to him. I got pretty wet, and as it was a very cold day I rode to the town for some stimulants. I got a small glass of whisky, for which I paid one dollar, and I said to the landlord: "It tastes like turpentine." He said: "It is pine top." They cut off the boughs of pine and put them into the whisky to color it and give it strength; hence the name "pine top."

I reached my destination without further mishap, and after a few days' rest carried my piece of jeans to the tailor at Columbia, and soon I was the best-dressed soldier in Buckingham county. The night for the wedding soon drew near, and what a repast there was! There were on the table all shapes of cake —tea, pound, and sponge cake—but all made of the same ingredients, flour and sorghum. The coffee was made of parched rye mixed with parched sweet potato peelings and sweetened with sorghum. I do not believe that, in January, 1864, there were more than five bags of coffee in Virginia. Nearly all the saddles had been denuded of their skirts to make soles for shoes; and when leather gave out, the farmers blocked out of hickory or dogwood solid soles and heels. By taking sheepskin for uppers, it gave a solid hair shoe, comfortable to ride in but very hard on the feet and limbs in walking. The negro boy who made my fire woke me up by his tramping upstairs like a horse. Of course in riding horseback the wooden shoes were all right.

I was struck with the absence of young men. They were all at the front with General Lee. The old men and women, the girls and boys, were at home, and the slaves watched over and guarded those girls as if they were their own children. I never heard of an improper act committed anywhere in old Virginia by any of the old-time slaves. All honor to these old trusted servants, many of whom sleep in the sacred dust of old Virginia! Another thing that impressed me was the devotion of the Southern women to the boys in the army. They would deny themselves any little delicacy they could get to send to the boys, and they would knit and knit, sew and sew from morning till night; and as scarce as was cotton goods in 1864, I have seen the women tear up their skirts and make them into bandages and send them to our wounded in hospitals in Richmond.

The nearest male relatives I had at that time were three first cousins. Two of them had been discharged, and the other was in Company C, commanded by Captain Miller, and was in the Forty-fourth Virginia Regiment, General Jones's Brigade, Major General Edward Johnson's Division, Army of Northern Virginia; and I desired to be with my cousin in the final struggle. Being a native of Virginia, I was entitled to the transfer under certain conditions: (1) The assent of the captain commanding my company; (2) the consent of the captain of the company to which I wished to be transferred; (3) the approval of the Congressman representing my Congressional district.

Armed with these papers, I went to Richmond, and stopped at the Spottswood Hotel, next day sending my card to Hon. Thomas S. Bocock. He invited me to his room, where I explained to him my mission by saying that I wished to come back to my native state and try to defend her against the encroachments of General Grant. Mr. Bocock slapped me on the shoulder and said: "Young man, we would like to have twenty thousand like you. We will go down to the War Department, where we will meet Mr. Judah P. Benjamin, and will arrange the transfer for you." We had a pleasant meeting with Mr. Benjamin, who was then acting in place of Mr. Seddon. Mr. Benjamin said that I would have to return to the First Tennessee Regiment at Dalton, and the transfer would reach me through the headquarters of General Joseph E. Johnston. On my return to Dalton the regiment was in comfortable winter quarters, but I was very lonely. Only nine of my old Company B were present, and I was glad a few days after to get notice to report to Captain Miller, Company C, Forty-fourth Virginia Regiment, on the Rapidan, near Vedersville, Va. As General Lee's army was in winter quarters, and I did not have to report in any specified time, I returned to Virginia, and went over much the same ground as previously, except that I made the trip by canal. I visited also while in Lynchburg. I arrived at Orange Courthouse March 14, 1864, on quite a cold night. I went to the only hotel near the depot, which was covered with what are called in Virginia "clapboards." I was surprised on awaking next morning to find about three inches of snow on my coverlet. It had drifted in under the boards. I found outside about ten inches of snow, through which I had to trudge ten miles before I found my regiment.

CHAPTER VII.

ON THE RAPIDAN.

I FOUND my boys in a comfortable cabin, ten of them in my cousin's mess. He was just recovering from a wound received at Brandy Station. I was considered as a guest of the boys, and did not have to go through any drudgery such as cooking or washing. However, I was detailed on picket duty, and occasionally on drill. When I reached the camp, rations consisted of middling meat and corn bread, without any salt. We got along without salt as long as the middling meat lasted, as that was quite salty. By the 1st of May the meat was gone, and many of the soldiers were without shoes. When the meat gave out, we resorted to wild onions, which were plentiful in that section, but hard to dig up. They were about the size of shallots, but very deep rooted, and we had to dig pretty deep with bayonets to get them up. These onions and corn bread without salt did very well toward appeasing the appetite of hungry soldiers.

One day I was on picket duty near the Rapidan River, which is a stream a little larger than Duck River in Tennessee; just opposite us were the Yankee pickets. One of them yelled out: "Hello, Johnny Reb! how is sassafras tea to-day?" I told him the tea was all right, but we had no sugar. I asked him how he was fixed for tobacco, and he said, "Very short"; so we arranged on the morrow to get on duty again. I was to bring a plug of tobacco, and he a shot pouch of coffee. The Federals had their coffee parched, ground, and sugar mixed with it; so on the morrow we made the exchange, and I don't think that I ever enjoyed coffee as much as I did that, having been months without a taste of pure coffee. After making the exchange, he asked me how I would like to have a New York *Herald*. He said that it was not contraband, for it was several weeks old. I told him that I would like very much to see it, as we did not get any papers now, and the ones received were printed on the reverse side of wall paper and were so flimsy that they would not stand the mails. So he tied the *Herald* to a stick and threw it across to me. When I opened it up, I read as follows: *"The Rebel Capital Must be Captured at All Hazards; General Grant Has Been Appointed to the Task."* He afterwards uttered what became a memorable saying: "I will fight it out on this line if it takes all summer."

CHAPTER VIII.

The Wilderness Campaign.

On May 1 General Lee issued the following order: "Send all extra baggage to the rear"; and on May 3 he issued an order to cook three days' rations. The first order was easily complied with. Back to Buckingham county was sent my Baltimore coat. The second order was also easily complied with. Three days' rations were three pones of corn bread without any sifting and minus salt. We did not have any sifters in General Lee's army; and if we had, we could not have afforded the loss of the bran.

On the night of May 4, 1864, General Grant crossed the Rapidan at Germana, United States, and Ely's fords. We had advanced to Mine Run, and on the night of the 4th the two armies were not far apart. The Wilderness is a peculiar country, and in the early days much gold ore was smelted there. From the Rapidan to Spottsylvania Courthouse, fourteen miles, is the wilderness proper. It is a slightly undulating country without hills, but abounds in the thickest growth of pine or black-jack. The pines are very tall, and range from an inch to twelve inches in diameter. These small pines grow in thickets, and in some places it is difficult to walk through. Sometimes you can walk a mile through nothing but a wilderness of pines, with now and then a black-jack; then it reverses, and you can walk for a mile in a wilderness of black-jack, with now and then a pine. The growth was thus because in cutting timber in the early days for smelting the undergrowth came up afterwards as described. There were very few cleared fields in this section, and they took their names from their owners.

General Grant's headquarters on the night of May 4 were near the Wilderness Tavern, and one mile and a half from Palmer's old field; and our line of pickets was on the edge of Palmer's field. A few years ago I was where General Grant pitched his tent at the Wilderness. The trees were then standing between which he rested the night of May 4, after crossing the Rapidan, which was less than a mile distant. That night everything betokened the conflict on the coming morrow—the neighing of the horses, the unlimbering of artillery, the commands of the officers, could be distinctly heard from our lines.

Before taps one of General Grant's bands struck up the old song once revered by North and South alike:

> The star-spangled banner, long may it wave
> O'er the land of the free and the home of the brave!

The music echoed and reëchoed through that wilderness of pines, and our band responded with that song so dear to Southern hearts:

> Hurrah, hurrah, for Southern rights hurrah!
> Hurrah for the bonnie blue flag that bears a single star.

In response to our "Bonnie Blue Flag" General Grant's band played "Home, Sweet Home." Looking back to that scene of May 4, 1864, I have often thought that if the messenger of peace could have hovered over the camp that night many would have been saved to family and friends; for between May 5 and 12 nearly fifty thousand men fell, General Grant losing nearly forty thousand. General Lee being on the defensive, his loss was only about ten thousand.

What a contrast between the two armies assembled on the night of May 4, 1864! General Grant's army numbered about one hundred and seventeen thousand, and it was the best equipped and best provisioned army ever marshaled in the United States. On the other hand, General Lee had only about fifty-five thousand ill clad and poorly fed men, but they were veterans who had previously held at bay such generals as McClellan, Meade, Hooker, and Burnside. Many of the men were nearly barefooted; and some were just from the hospital, with their wounds not yet healed. The morning of May 5, 1864, found us forming on the old plank road, my regiment extending across it. There were two roads extending from Orange Courthouse to Fredericksburg, thirty-two miles distant. One was called the plank road and the other the dirt road. Both led out of Orange Courthouse together, but diverged soon after. At our line they were three miles apart, and it was sixteen miles by each road to Orange Courthouse or Fredericksburg. The plank road was nearest the Rapidan River, and our left rested not far from the river (our line extended three miles), the right resting on the dirt road near Parker's store. Running from the Rapidan River and crossing the plank road and dirt road was the Brock road, extending from the Rapidan River to Spottsylvania Courthouse, eighteen miles from the Rapidan River. General Lee made no resistance to the passage of General Grant across the Rapidan; in fact, all our pickets had been withdrawn when General Grant first reached and obtained possession of the Brock road. He thought that General Lee was retiring toward Richmond, but we were hid in the Wilderness for the time being. His scouts reported our whereabouts after nightfall of May 4. On the morning of May 5 we were forming our lines; and as General Grant's numbers outflanked us, we had to stretch out the thin gray line, and on my part of the line we did not have a rear rank, and the front rank files were so far apart that they could not touch elbows. My line of battle was in a pine thicket on the edge of Palmer's field, a clearing of some two hundred feet in width and some five hundred feet in length. On General Grant's side of the field the pine and underbrush were as thick as on our side. Just in the rear of our line, and running parallel with us, was a newly cut road on which wagons had recently been hauling out timber. Into this road we ran a battery of nine pieces charged with grape and canister. This was our position when, about 3 P.M., the picket lines commenced firing, and our pickets, who were across the old field, ran to and joined our ranks. Soon a line of blue appeared on the opposite side of the thicket and opened a brisk fire, and continued to advance on us; and the battle of the Wilderness had begun. The One Hundred and Forty-sixth New York Zouaves were in our immediate front, and their commander was Major Gilbert. They were as fine-looking a body of men as I ever saw. They had yellow sashes around their waists, red caps with tassels, and leggings on their ankles. With our shots and those from the nine pieces of artillery they were mowed down like grass before the sickle. It appeared to me that the whole regiment was annihilated. Another line appeared quickly to take their place, and the battle waged hot and fast till toward nightfall, when General Grant withdrew his line into the thicket; and all through the night we lay on our arms expecting an attack, as the artillery he had placed some distance off boomed at us unceasingly. On the morning of May 6 eleven hundred Federals were dead on Palmer's old field. All their haversacks had disappeared, and in many instances their knapsacks, and the pockets of each were turned inside out, showing that their pockets had been picked. Our men threw away their rations of corn bread, as they had three days' rations of hard-tack, besides some bacon and coffee. When the Federals made their last charge, we were lying down firing, and after they retired I said to my cousin, who was by my side: "That was an impetuous charge." Hearing no response from him, I looked and saw that a bullet had pierced his forehead, killing him instantly. I wrapped him in his oilcloth and blanket, and with the assistance of comrades buried him with a black-jack tree for his headstone, into which I cut with a knife the initials of his name, then wrote to his father telling him the spot in case he wished him removed to the old family burying ground, near Buckingham Church. Some months after, I received a letter from his father saying: "My son died like a true soldier on the field of battle, and I shall there let his bones rest."

After burying all of our dead, Lieutenant George

Price, of my company, and I were sitting on a pine log to rest. All around was quiet except now and then a shot from sharpshooters. We were only a short distance from their line, and could see the Federal dead in the old field. We were talking of the dead boys, and the feelings of the folks at home when the news should reach them, when suddenly I heard a thud, and saw the blood gushing from above the heart of my lieutenant. I gathered him in my arms and lowered him to the earth. He did not speak, but from his inside pocket gave me a daguerreotype. On opening the case I saw the fair features of a James River young lady, and one whom I had heard play and sing "When This Cruel War Is Over."

On the morning of May 6 about sunrise one of our boys came into the lines with a pair of boots on his arm. He said that he had been trying all night to get the boots, but that every time he attempted to pull them off the soldier would open his eyes. He died just before this, and our comrade got the boots.

All day quiet reigned in our front, save now and then the sharpshooters of the enemy, who fired from the tall trees; but of course their shots were at random, as we could not be seen from their lines. On the right of our line the battle was raging furiously. General Grant threw the columns of General Warren against those of Longstreet, and attempted to turn our right flank as he had failed the previous day to turn our left. The battle was in a wilderness of black-jacks as thick as ours was of pines. First one side and then the other advanced and receded till the end of the day's struggle, when General Longstreet held the ground in advance of where it commenced. Eight years ago, when I was going over the Wilderness battlefield, I came upon a huge stone which marked the spot where one of the Texas Rangers took hold of the bridle reins of "Traveler" and carried General Lee from the front to the rear.

The 7th of May was very quiet and quite warm. The bodies of the dead in the old field were very much swollen, and General Lee sent a flag of truce to General Grant requesting that we be allowed to bury the Federal dead, which request was granted. There is very little ceremony in burying the dead of an enemy. With a shovel the dirt is removed the length of the soldier and to the depth of eight or ten inches, and then with the shovel the body is turned into the little trench, sometimes falling on side or back and sometimes on the face; the dirt removed from the little trench is then shoveled onto the body, and is soon washed off by the rains, when the body is mutilated by hogs or vultures. We had buried but few of the dead when orders came to fall into ranks, as General Grant was on the march toward Richmond. As we were in the rear, our march was very slow, and we soon bivouacked for the night.

On May 8 we passed near where Generals Warren and Longstreet fought on the 6th, and saw many sickening sights. The wads from the guns had fired the thick beds of leaves in the black-jack thicket, and some of our wounded had been burned, and their charred remains were close to our line of march. We moved very slowly on the 9th of May; but on the 10th, early in the morning, our advance was in position a few miles northeast of Spottsylvania Courthouse, and General Grant made a furious charge, trying to dislodge us, but General Lee held the position. General Sedgwick was killed, and near by is a handsome monument erected to him. On the night of May 10, by the aid of engineers' voices (it was a very dark night), the dead angle was formed, and we commenced to dig lively with our bayonets, throwing out the dirt with tin plates. On the night of May 11 the trench was completed and occupied by us, as we expected an attack at any moment. In building the trench we threw the dirt out in front, and on top of the dirt placed some small pine logs, cut out of the thicket. The logs would be of no use in case artillery was used, but we knew that General Grant could not use it on account of the wilderness, but the little logs served their purpose in catching Minie balls. All night there was a steady drizzling rain, and soon after daylight on the morning of the 12th of May we heard the pickets firing, and soon they came running in and scampered over the breastworks and yelled out, "Boys, the Yanks are coming in three columns!" and soon we were engaged with General Hancock's Corps. The battle raged furiously for a while, and the front column of the Federals was not more than thirty feet from our line. Soon I heard one of our men say: "Stop firing; they will kill all of us." I heard a voice in our rear say, "Surrender," and it was accompanied with an oath. I looked up, and General Thomas Francis Meagher's Brigade was in our rear, and some of our men were being shot and clubbed to death with guns after they had thrown down their arms. The big, burly Irishman that had called on me to surrender had his gun within two feet of my body and his finger on the trigger. Why he did not shoot, I will never know. Major General Edward Johnson, commanding my division, and Colonel Norvell Cobbs, of my regiment, had dismounted previous to the battle, and were near me in the trenches, and we leaped the breastworks, grabbing the pine logs on top to assist us over, and we were in the midst of the attacking column in front. Eleven hundred men were captured, which comprised all of General Johnson's division except seven of my regiment that were on our extreme right. When we reached General Hancock's men they displayed the excitement incident to a fierce charge, and I think we had about four guards to each prisoner. They rushed to us and said, "To the rear, quick, men"; and away they ran with us. Of course we know that it was not our personal safety that they were looking after, but they wished to get out of the fight. After the war I talked with one of the seven men who was not captured, and he said that just after we left the trenches General J. B. Gordon came up with his division, and charged Meagher's Brigade, tumbling them into the trenches that we had left and, crossing them, was soon in the midst of Hancock's Corps, whose ranks had been so depleted by his men going with us to the rear that a gap was left in front. It was in this charge that General Gordon caught the bridle rein of Traveler and asked General Lee to retire to the rear, as his boys would do the fighting. Our three or four guards each trotted us to the rear rapidly, and I suspect would have gone with

us as far as Fredericksburg, but for General Grant;
for when we reached his headquarters, about a mile
in the rear, the General was directing couriers to different positions on the field. When he saw the head
column of prisoners attended by so many guards, he
knew why there was trouble in General Hancock's
ranks. Turning to one of his staff, General Grant
said: "Reorganize that line; for every four prisoners a
guard, and place Lieutenant —————— in command."
When the line was reorganized, we proceeded slowly
along the dirt road in single file toward the town of
Fredericksburg, distant sixteen miles. Soon we had
to move out of the road and take to the edge of the
woods, for marching in columns of fours were twenty-
five thousand soldiers who had been doing duty as
guards since we invaded Pennsylvania and Maryland.
Many of them were members of the heavy artillery,
and had been armed as infantrymen. Each regiment was headed by a fine band. We were in a sorry
plight to meet such an array of tinseled regalia. Many
of our men were hatless, shoeless, and coatless, and
were covered with mud from the trenches. This
grand army guyed us all day. As we met one column a good-natured-looking soldier yelled out: "Hello, Johnnies! we are taking you North, and will give
you something to eat, put some clothes on your backs,
and shoes on your feet."

Toward nightfall we bivouacked on the marshy
plains of Marye Heights, overlooking Fredericksburg.
The ground was wet and marshy. One of our boys had
a pocketknife, and we cut some chinquapin bushes, and
four of us set back to back on the pile of bushes,

This was a good way to rest and sleep when the wet ground would not allow a horizontal position. We had a chain picket around our camp. In army par-

THE BIVOUAC

lance a chain picket is one in which the guards are so close together that with extended arms they can touch hands; so it would be difficult to get away with guards so near each other.

The next day we went through Fredericksburg, crossed the Rappahannock River on the pontoon General John Pope built while he was in the campaign of "On to Richmond, with headquarters in the saddle." Eight miles from Fredericksburg we reached Belle Plains, on the Potomac. We camped a few days here, waiting for transports, and drew very good rations of hard-tack, bacon, sugar, and coffee. Here I first saw what was then termed the Christian Commission, whose duty it was to minister to the spiritual and ma-. terial welfare of the United States Army. They did not minister to any of the Confederate prisoners. I guess they thought we were an incorrigible set.

CHAPTER IX.

Prison Life, Point Lookout, Md.

In a few days the transports came along, and we
boarded them quickly, reaching Point Lookout May
20; and before getting in line each prisoner was sub-

IN THE HANDS OF COLORED TROOPS.

jected to a search and relieved of any valuables or
knives and pistols. We found as guards here about
eleven hundred colored soldiers, in command of
Major H. G. O. Weymouth, of the Nineteenth Mas-

sachusetts Regiment. Major Weymouth lost a leg in the battle of Fredericksburg, and this post was given him, and also because he was a good executive officer.

General Grant knew how to economize in men; and as these colored soldiers had not behaved well at the front, he replaced them with white troops and sent the colored soldiers to Point Lookout. This camp occupied some twenty acres of sandy land. It was a peninsula with several wells, and the waters before the war were noted for their medicinal properties. It was situated on Chesapeake Bay at the confluence of the Potomac River. The bay was twenty-five miles wide, and it was eight miles across the Potomac. The camp was surrounded by a fence sixteen feet high, and three feet from the top was a parapet walkway which was the beat of the guards, who were stationed some forty feet apart; besides, there were also a garrison on the outside and artillery, shotted, to be used in case of an insurrection by the prisoners.

Much has been said, written, and spoken of the treatment of prisoners, North and South. In the United States Senate it was on one occasion the cause of a heated debate between Senators Hill and Blaine; and no doubt Senator Hill got the better of the argument, for with the Southern ports all blockaded, our people raising tobacco, cotton, resin, and turpentine, we did not have provisions to feed the army, and consequently the prisoners at Andersonville and other Southern prisons had to fare the same as our army. On the other hand, the United States was teeming with men, provisions, and money, all the ports were open to the world, and a bounty of six hundred dollars had induced a great flood of emigrants from the Old World. While the words I use in describing prison life may be harsh, yet there is no bitterness in my heart. When I took the oath of allegiance at Elmira, N. Y., nearly three months after General Lee surrendered, I turned my back upon the past, and buried it with all its prejudices and animosities. I recognize the fatherhood of God, the brotherhood of man, and there is no one with whom I cannot clasp hands.

The quarters at Point Lookout were large Sibley tents, which were cone-shaped. These tents would accommodate seventeen men sleeping in a circle. We did not need any blankets, and for a pillow we raked up a bank of sand. It was very hot in these tents with so many bunkmates. Our rations consisted of salt pork, bean soup, hard-tack, and occasionally fresh meat. We had not been in prison long before we were deprived of coffee. There were three large gates in the fence opening out to Chesapeake Bay, and we bathed and did our washing there. Near Major Weymouth's headquarters was another gate, opening to the pier where all the vessels unloaded prisoners and supplies. On the bay side at night the gates were closed, and no one could get to the bay. I was at the Point five weeks without change of clothing. I would go into the bay, wash my clothes, hang them on sand to dry, and go into the water up to my chin to keep from getting sunburned. At the end of five weeks I resolved to get some clothing, so I denied myself a ration a day, and after the two days' fast I sold my two rations to a fellow-prisoner for five cents, and with the money I purchased from the sutler one postage stamp, in those days three cents, and one cent each for sheets of paper and envelopes; and as soon as my letter reached a friend in Baltimore he sent me a package of clothing and a ten-pound package of Killi-kinnick smoking tobacco. In writing a letter you could use only one side of the sheet, as all letters had to be examined and approved before mailing, and you had to be careful not to write anything contraband. The envelopes were stamped: "Prisoner's letter, examined and approved." On receiving letters, they first came to the commandant and were read and stamped approved by him. Remittances of money, by mail or express, were receipted for by the commandant, and then turned over to the sutler. In some prisons I have heard that the commandant and sutler were partners; I do not think that this was the case, however, at Point Lookout. At nine o'clock at night the bugle was sounded for taps or lights out, and every one had to be in his tent at that hour with lights out. The colored soldiers patroled after nine o'clock along the avenues between the tents with six-shooters in their hands; and if they heard any noise in a tent, they would shoot into it; therefore, after 9 P.M. Point Lookout, with its army of ten thousand men, was almost as quiet as a cemetery.

Of course it was very humiliating to Southern men to be thus guarded by some of their former slaves. All the commissaries, wood, etc., was unloaded by details of prisoners; and many of them were anxious to get on this detail, as it gave them a day outside of prison walls, and also sometimes an opportunity to appropriate some extra rations; and again, they could hear what they called grapevine news. Newspapers were not allowed in the prison, and our chance to hear anything from the front was very limited. There was a line inside the prison called the dead line, which was one of the guards' beats, and no one was allowed to cross this line. One evening a squad which had been on detail on the outside entered the prison, and quite a crowd rushed up to them to hear the news, and some of them were crowded over the dead line. Without hesitation the guard fired into the group, severely wounding two of our prisoners. Major Weymouth had the sentinel removed, but I never heard of his court-martial. Our ears were frequently greeted with the expression from the colored guards: "The bottom rail is on top now; my gun wants to smoke."

For a great deal of persecution from the guards I do not think that Major Weymouth was responsible. They were, nearly all of them, young negroes from the North Carolina tobacco fields. They were uniformed the same as white troops, and of course they felt their importance. While Major Weymouth was at the head of the troops, he was also to command the prisoners and to see that there was no infringement of the rules and regulations. Major Weymouth was a Mason, and allowed the prisoners to make an appeal to the fraternity at Baltimore for clothing, which was sent to the prison, and he distributed it to them.

Major Wirz occupied the same position at Andersonville in command of our guards, who were all white. There is no doubt that many indignities offered prisoners at Andersonville were without his knowledge or consent. Mr. Oakley, who is at present yardmaster of the Louisville and Nashville Railroad, was from an Ohio regiment, and served a term in Andersonville. I heard him say that Wirz was a Mason, and that he had known him on many occasions to read the Masonic burial service over his dead. Mr. Oakley contends that Wirz was not a cruel man, yet the poor fellow was denied the glorious death of a soldier by being shot, but suffered an ignominious death by hanging. If we had gained our independence, I do not think that Major Weymouth would have been hanged for the may crimes committed by the colored sentinels at Point Lookout; but there is no telling what feelings are engendered by a civil war in which father is arrayed against son, brother against brother, and neighbor against neighbor. We lived too close to our brethren in East Tennessee and Kentucky not to be familiar with the bitter sectional hate; but let me digress just here to give an illustration between a civil and a foreign war, in which the treatment of prisoners of war is in marked contrast. During the Spanish-American War I was in Norfolk, Va., just after one hundred and twenty prisoners had been received at the Naval Hospital from Admiral Cervera's fleet. Our ladies were very kind to them, sending them all sorts of delicacies; and it will be remembered that some enthusiastic American suggested that we purchase a mansion for the Admiral, and induce him to reside with us.

A peculiar malady affected the prisoners at Point Lookout. After dark about half of them were blind, and daylight would restore their sight. One day I asked the doctor the cause, and he said that he thought that the salty soup mixed with the mineral water had something to do with it, but that the prime cause was the sun's heat and reflection from the water, the sand, and the white tents.

One day there was quite a commotion in camp, and I saw a crowd gathering near one of the tents. On inquiry I heard, "There is a woman in camp." It appeared that, in order to be with her lover, who was an artilleryman, she had doffed her feminine garb, cut short her hair, and donned the uniform of an artilleryman. Major Weymouth provided her with feminine wearing apparel and sent her home. Whether either survived the cruel war and afterwards married, "this deponent sayeth not."

An enterprising prisoner whom I knew many years ago in Lynchburg, Va., made him a gambling house of pieces of cracker boxes, and here gambling was going on from early morn till nearly nine o'clock at night. If the prisoners did not have any money, they put up tobacco as stakes.

In July, 1864, the prison was overcrowded with captures from General's Lee's army, and the government was building a new one at Elmira, N. Y., and about the 15th of July commenced to transfer a large number to that point. I left July 30 on a transport. One thousand men were loaded on one steamer. We were packed away in the hull and lower deck, and

were not allowed in the cabin. We steamed down
the bay, and were en route to Jersey City. Before
reaching Elmira it may be well to give some statistics :

White troops enlisted by the United States 1861-65,
    about 2,100,000
Colored troops.................................... 190,000
The Confederate States, about..................... 650,000
The United States captured........................ 220,000
The Confederate States captured................... 270,000
Died in Northern prisons..........................   26,246
Died in Southern prisons..........................   22,576

The death rate North was twelve per cent., while the
death rate South was only nine per cent., and we have
already seen that there was little in the South to feed
prisoners or any one else. When we landed at Jersey
City, I saw a large crowd over at Governor's Island,
and upon inquiring who they were, the answer came :
"Bounty jumpers." I asked what constituted a bounty
jumper, and the reply was that a lot of foreigners
came to the United States for the six hundred dollars
bounty, and after getting the money deserted.

Soon after reaching Jersey City we disembarked,
and were loaded into the cars, and a guard stationed
at each door. The car windows were small, and there
was no chance to get out. While en route we were not
allowed to speak to any one at the various stations at
which we stopped.

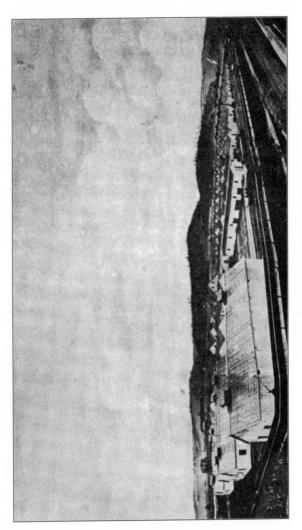

PRISON CAMP, ELMIRA, N. Y.

CHAPTER X.

Prison Life at Elmira, N. Y.

We reached Elmira prison August 2, 1864, and as we marched through the city quite a curious crowd followed us and commented on the appearance of the Rebels, as they termed us. We had been preceded by some fifteen hundred prisoners from the former prison at Point Lookout. As Elmira was a new prison, the government had not built any barracks, and we were comfortably quartered in tents; and the tents were located some fifty feet from the stockade, and no one was allowed to go between the tents and fence or stockade.

The prison camp contained some forty acres of land about one mile above the city, and near the Cheming River, a beautiful, clear, limpid mountain stream of very pure water. The stockade that surrounded the camp was much like the one at Point Lookout, but built of heavier material, and the ends of the upright planks going some eighteen inches into the ground. The planks were about sixteen feet high, and nailed to heavy sills, which were supported by large posts set deep in the ground. The stockade was about sixteen feet high, and three feet from the top was the parapet walkway or beat of the guards, who were stationed some forty feet apart, and were relieved every two hours by other guards. Commencing at nine o'clock at night, or at taps, they would cry out their posts all through the hours of the night, as, "Post No. 1, nine o'clock; all is well," which would be taken up by all posts, and repeated all around the stockade. Inside the stockade, about fifty feet apart, were large coal oil lamps nailed near the center of the stockade, with large reflectors, which were lit after nightfall, and the guards on the parapet would be able to see any one approaching.

The tents in which we slept were struck every morning in order for inspection. The prisoners in one of the tents had a false floor laid and covered with dirt hard packed so it would have the same appearance as the ground floor in the other tents. Under this false floor was one of the prisoners, digging day and night. There were six occupants of this particular tent, and by making a detail one man was digging all the time. They were tunneling to get under the fence. The tunnel was only about two feet under the ground, and they had to go about sixty feet distance to get under the fence; the only implement they had was a large knife. They had a small box to which was attached a string at both ends, and when the fellow at the farther side had filled his box he gave a pull of the string, and the other fellow just under the false floor of the tent would pull the box under the floor, pile up the dirt, and at night they would remove the false floor, gather the dirt in their hands, fill their haversacks, and scatter the dirt along the new-made streets. When they reached the upright planks of the stockade they had to go over a foot lower than the tunnel in order to get under the end of the planks. Finally the tunnel was completed, and one of the boys crawled through, poked his head on the outside, and came and reported bright moonshine, disclosed the camp of the guards under patrol across the street, and a number of pieces of artillery in position along the camp; so they waited for the moon to go down before they commenced their underground journey. The plan was that the last of the six to leave should notify as many of the prisoners as he could, in order that they might take advantage of it; but only fifteen got out, and we heard that they reached Canada in safety.

I had charge of and was sergeant, by Federal appointment, of Ward Thirty-six. My duty was to call the roll once a day, make out the daily ration report, and to report the sick sent to the hospital and convalescents received from the hospital. While out calling the roll the morning the boys made their escape, I saw a number of the guards with picks in their hands, and they excavated the tunnel up to the tent and carried away and destroyed the false bottom. I was surprised to see how crooked the tunnel was, yet underground it was so dark that they could not make it straight. The tunneling ceased after that successful attempt.

It is fortunate that I kept a diary in Elmira prison, which refreshes memory of the many scenes I witnessed during my sojourn there, and the following survivors of the camp are now living and can testify to my statements: Alphonso S. Allen, Nashville, Tenn.; L. T. Webb, Nashville, Tenn.; R. W. Miller, Nashville, Tenn.; W. S. Riddle, Nashville, Tenn.; W. G.

Lloyd, Lewisburg, Tenn.; P. D. Houston, Lewisburg, Tenn.; D. B. Anderson, Gallatin, Tenn.; H. M. Cartmell, Lebanon, Tenn.; Stokely Jacobs, Murfreesboro, Tenn.; Richard Messick, Beech Grove, Tenn.

In a military prison it was very difficult to get information from the outside world. No papers were allowed, and the papers received had been opened and read; if there was anything contraband, you did not get it. When you wrote a letter it was left unsealed, and when the prison authorities examined it they stamped it "Prisoner's letter, approved," and then sealed and mailed it. Money was contraband of war, for a fellow might bribe his way out; therefore, whenever a remittance came to a prisoner it was turned over to the sutler, who opened an account with the owner, and he could purchase all he wished so long as the funds held out; but when money went, a prisoner's credit was *non est*.

Until I reached prison I did not know what a slave to habit man was. I have seen men go hungry a day and save their rations and trade them for tobacco. I have seen a prisoner discharge a quid of tobacco from his mouth and another one pick it up, dry and smoke it. They used the black navy tobacco, sold in prison at the rate of one dollar per pound. They would cut it into little squares; each square would be called a chew, and five chews five cents. We had all kinds of trades and traffics, and tobacco was one of the mediums of exchange. We had many barbers, and they would shave you for five chews of tobacco. When the barber would get more tobacco than he needed, he would sell five chews for a small loaf of bread, valued at five cents, or he could purchase a small piece of meat or a fresh rat, each valued at five cents. These barbers carried square boxes with them, upon which they set their patients; and a fellow would have to be very patient, as they never used a hone or strap except their boots and shoes, and it was hard to tell

SHAVE FOR FIVE CHEWS OF TOBACCO.

which was the worst sufferer, the barber or his customer.

Before the fall season opened the government had erected forty-two wards, capable of holding and sleeping three hundred men each, with bunks three

high on each side; also two large hospitals, and one
large cook house where the light bread was baked
and soup and meat cooked. Adjoining the cook house
was a large shed with tables that would accommodate three hundred men, and there were in the shed
about twenty tables which were higher than my waist
when standing. Of course they were higher to a
small boy. Seats were not allowed. The men were
marched in in two ranks, and separated at the head
of the table, making one rank face the other. Each
man had a plate and spoon; in the plate were his bean
soup and beans, by the side of his plate was a small
piece of light bread, and on the bread a thin ration of
salt pork. The rations were thus prepared: A baker
who lived outside would come in daily and superin-
tend the baking. In the cook house were a large number of iron kettles or caldrons in which the meat and
beans were boiled. I suppose these caldrons would
hold fifty gallons. The salt pork was shipped in
barrels and rolled up to the caldrons, and with a
pitchfork tossed in, then the beans—I have heard the
boys say four beans to a gallon of water. Now when
this is boiled down it gets very salty, and after three
weeks of a diet of this kind a prisoner will commence
to get sick. I thought for a while that the government
was retaliating on us on account of Andersonville, but
I afterwards believed that it was done by the army
contractors. We had the same kind of a scandal in the
corned beef business during the Spanish-American
War; we would nowadays call them grafters. So I
can say without hesitancy that the death rate here was

higher than at any other prison North or South. The life of the prison did not average seven months, because it was not opened till July, 1864, and prisoners arrived till December, 1864, when the maximum of twelve thousand had been received. There are two thousand nine hundred and seventeen graves in the cemetery,

THE BARREL SHIRT.

and over two thousand died who were exchanged to go home and die, and many died before they reached home. A prisoner eating this diet will crave any kind of fresh meat. Marching through the camp one day was a prisoner in a barrel shirt, with placard, "I eat a dog"; another one bearing a barrel, with placard, "Dog Eater." The barrel shirt was one of the modes of punishment. The shirt was made by using a whisky or coal oil barrel, knocking out one end and in the other boring a hole so as to get the head through, and then putting on a placard to indicate the crime. It appeared that these prisoners had captured a lapdog owned by the baker who came into camp daily to bake the bread. The baker made complaint to Colonel Beall, and said that his wife and children would not have taken one hundred dollars for the dog. As the prisoners had nothing to pay with, they were treated to the barrel shirt. The punishment was a two hours' march followed by a soldier with a bayonet, and they were not allowed much rest till the two hours were completed. I saw another barrel shirt, "I told a lie." A prisoner did not have much compunction of conscience, especially if he had lied to deceive the commandant, which he conceived to be his religious duty. A prisoner carrying a barrel shirt, "I stole my messmate's rations," was hissed all around the camp; and deservedly so, because a man who would steal from his messmates in prison deserved the most severe punishment; while the ones who carried the placard "Dog Eater" had the sympathies of the entire camp, because many of them would have enjoyed a piece of the fresh meat. When twitted about it, they said: "It was not a common cur, but a Spitz, and tasted like mutton."

On account of the waste from the commissary a great many rodents from Elmira ran into the prison. As there were not any holes in which they could hide, it was an easy catch for the boys by knocking them

over with sticks, and there was quite a traffic in them.
As there was very little currency in prison, tobacco,
rats, pickles, pork, and light bread were mediums of
exchange.   Five chews of tobacco would buy a rat, a
rat would buy five chews of tobacco, a loaf of bread
would buy a rat, a rat would buy a loaf of bread, and
so on.   I am glad that I did not have to go on this

TRAFFIC IN RODENTS.

diet; but I have tasted a piece of rat, and it is much
like squirrel.   I bought one for one of my men who
was sick.   I had friends in Louisville, Cincinnati, Baltimore, Hoosick Falls, N. Y., and was kept well supplied with everything I needed until an order was issued saying that we would have to get a permit to

ask for anything in the North. I suppose this was done because we were arousing too much sympathy. When cut off from the North, I fell back on Nashville friends. On August 19, 1864, the sutler received orders not to sell us any fruits or vegetables, but it was rescinded in about two weeks. In the meantime I was prepared for it. I had sent out and bought a

THE DYING PRISONER.

sheet-iron stove and had it erected in my office, which was a room about eight by ten in the front end of the ward. I had three bunks, and three of the boys stayed with me. One did the cooking, one the washing, and the other attended to the sick in the ward; and by reference to my diary I find that I weighed, on the cookhouse scales, one hundred and eighty-one pounds. As sergeant of the ward I had to make the requisitions for rations for the ward, also for the sick in the ward, and I rarely made a correct one, and the mistake was always in my favor, and the extra rations thus obtained sufficed for three of us. We would take the salt pork and give it about three boilings in fresh water together with the beans, and when fried the pork would taste like fresh meat; on account of the diet the hospitals were all filled, and many sick were in the wards. There was a young man named Stroup, from South Carolina. He was a nephew of Squire W. D. Robinson, of Nashville. I had been writing to the Squire for Stroup, and money was sent to him, and he had been examined by the doctor for exchange; but I was satisfied that he would not leave the prison alive, and one morning as I knelt by his bunk and pressed his clammy brow with my hard hand, he feebly said "Mother," and his soul passed into the beyond. But it was not mother's hand; mother was in the far Southland, and I thought, "O the power of a mother's love!" and when a child could forget a mother's love it would be below the instincts of a brute.

The bunks extended the length of the ward on each side, leaving an aisle in the center and two stoves in each ward, and the prisoners were not allowed to get very close to them in zero weather. With an open building, the heat was not very intense. The bunks were three high, and the boys occupying the top bunk had to do some climbing. They were wide enough to sleep two medium-sized men. Each one was allowed only a pair of blankets, and so had to sleep on the hard board; therefore, in extreme weather four slept in the space of two, using one pair of blankets to sleep on, which gave three for cover. Two of them slept with their heads toward the east, and two with heads toward the west, and of course had to be on their sides; and when ready to change positions, one would call out, "All turn to the right"; and the next call would be, "All turn to the left." The turns had to be made as stated, or there would be collisions. Of course the men did not disrobe in extreme cold weather, and on awakening in the morning their feet would be in each other's faces.

Comrade W. S. Riddle, of Nashville, had not been in prison very long, and did not know all the rules, and one day he got hold of a cracker box and was whittling off shavings when the sergeant came along and asked: "What are you doing?" Will replied: "I am trying to make a softer bed; that board nearly breaks my back." The sergeant said: "Throw out those shavings, sir; you are not allowed to litter up the ward." Not a straw or shaving was allowed in the ward. Each man was required to fold up his blanket in the morning and deposit it in the bunk. Comrade Riddle was horrified one day to see four prisoners sitting in a bunk playing poker, when in a near-by bunk was a dying prisoner. But such is war: a man's sensibilities are dwarfed. To illustrate the severity of prison life, Riddle went into Elmira with a squad of six, and he was the only one to get out alive. By reference to my diary, I note that we had almost daily inspection in the wards, and every ten days we had what the officers called "muster" on the outside. In the ward inspection the boys were formed in two ranks inward face, hat in hand, while the Federal inspection officer passed down one line and returned by the other. I think this was to keep the officer in military training. In the muster on the outside my diary says that on one occasion the boys were held in line two hours on a very cold day and in snow ankle-deep. This was very rough on the boys from the extreme South, and they shivered as with chills.

My diary says that Major Richmond ordered me to the guardhouse for throwing water on the street. The guardhouse was a room about forty feet square, without any light or ventilation; it was like a dungeon. I said to the guard: "Wait until I write a note to Major Colt." In this note I said: "Officer of the day, Major Richmond, ordered me to the guardhouse for throwing water on the street. It was not dirty water, but from the dipper, as I saw some sediment in it previous to drinking. I respectfully ask that you give me a hearing, that I may vindicate myself." I was in the guardhouse, or dungeon, only a few hours when Major Colt ordered my release.

One night the boom of cannon saluted our ears, and a solid shot passed through Ward No. 5, and came near hitting some of the occupants. I heard later that the boys were making a noise, and the artillerymen thought that an insurrection was brewing, and they wanted us to know that the artillery was in position and ten guns always shotted for an emergency.

No civilians were allowed in the prison except on

permit from the President or the Secretary of War, so an enterprising citizen with an eye to business erected across the street from the prison a large observatory, reached from below by winding stairs. He charged ten cents for admission, and kept the platform filled all day. His customers used spyglasses, and scrutinized the camp with much curiosity. I suppose they got their money's worth. The baker, the preacher, and Horace Greeley were the only visitors that I saw previous to the surrender of General Lee. Mr. Greeley made some sneering remark about Southern chivalry, so when the time came that I should choose between General Grant and Mr. Greeley for President I voted for General Grant. I thought it was a magnanimous act when he said, "Boys, take your horses, go home, and go to work"; and later, when the Federal authorities attempted to disturb the parole of General Lee, he said, "It cannot be done so long as I am in command of the army."

I find in my diary of November 8, 1864, the following entry: "The election appears to pass off quietly in Elmira; no demonstration at night. I believe it would be to the best interests of the South that old Abe be elected, because if General McClellan is elected it would tend to solidify the Northern Democrats." There was quite an anti-war party in the North, and we expected much disturbance at the November election, and there were local disturbances; but the government had so many soldiers at its command that all mobs were quickly dispersed.

I find in my diary of November 9, 1864: "Some of

the prisoners broke into the commissary last night and stole quite a lot of provisions, and an order was issued by Captain Whitson that if the provisions were not returned no more meals would be issued." It was roll call before the stolen articles were returned and we got our dinner.

On November 10 we had our regular muster, and

THE INGENIOUS PRISONER.

heard that President Lincoln was reëlected. In November, 1864, the boys commenced to get quite a lot of small change in the following way; and it illustrates that "necessity is the mother of invention," for without any previous knowledge the men engaged in the man-

ufacture of gutta-percha rings which were afterwards
sold and distributed throughout the North and South.
The machine with which the rings were made was a
simple one, and made with a knife. The upright or
drill was whittled out of a cracker box, and at the point
was a needle, a horizontal bar with a hole in the
center and a string tied at each end, the strings re-
versing at the top of the drill. Near the needle or drill
was a wheel which gave the drill a rotary action. By
moving the hand up and down the wheel moved forward and backward, drilling very rapidly. To get the
gutta-percha buttons, they approached the guards
quietly and said: "Bring us some gutta-percha buttons, and we will make you some rings; also bring in
some five- or ten-cent pieces of silver, so that we can
make settings for the rings." With a knife the inside of the button was cut out to fit the finger; then
with the drill two or three buttons were riveted together, and with a hammer the silver was flattened out
and cut with the knife into shapes of two hearts joined
together and two hands joined. In some instances
the men would get hold of a mussel shell highly colored, and insert a small seal in the ring. I have bought
and given away many of these rings, North and South,
and have some now in Nashville for which I paid two
dollars and a half. The next procedure was to dis-
pose of the rings, which was done by the guards smug-
gling them to the city, selling them, and dividing the
proceeds with the prisoners; and I believe in nearly
every instance the guards were honest in returning a
part of the proceeds of the sale. Generally their com-

missions were about one-half. There were also prisoners at work on horsehair watch guards or necklaces. They were made in a manner similar to the way that ladies work with a crochet needle, except the boys' needles were whittled out of pine. To make a hook, they cut out of a white beef bone a form representing a snake's head, and on top of this was carved a small dog or other animal in a sitting position. To the hook

THE BURIAL OF THE DEAD.

was attached a Bible in a small clasp. It was amusing to see men rob the horses' manes and tails to get the horsehair. These horses pulled the wagons that hauled the wood and commissaries inside the prison. Finally the horses were about to lose their hair appendages, and a guard was sent with each wagon.

The authorities at Elmira had an admirable system regarding the burial of the dead, and I have said that the care of the dead was better than that bestowed on the living. When a prisoner died, his name, company, and regiment were written on a slip of paper and pinned on the lapel of his coat. If he did not have a coat, it was pinned on his vest; and if the vest was gone, then it was pinned on the shirt. The body was removed to a house called the dead house, a building some thirty by forty feet in size. In this building were a large lot of boxes made out of poplar, not coffin-shaped, but straight boxes that resembled gun boxes; and into the box the body was deposited. On the lid of the box was nailed a headboard. The inscription was removed from the body, and copied in large letters —the name, company, regiment, and the date of death of deceased. The inscription was then put into a dry mineral-water bottle, corked perfectly tight, and placed under the armpit. Each grave was numbered, and an alphabetically arranged book kept in which the names were entered, and opposite the names were the numbers of the graves. In 1901 I stood by the graves of two thousand nine hundred and seventeen of our dead, and time had swept away each wooden headboard, but by digging into the graves I could have identified each body by the inscription in the mineral-water bottles.

From January 25 to January 29, 1865, there is not an entry in my diary. On the 29th of January, 1865, I find this entry: "On January 25, 1865, I was sent to the smallpox hospital, and returned on January 29, and the boys were all glad to see me." My experience as a smallpox patient was very trying. I was taken with a severe chill, with pains in my spine and back of my head. Comrade Stokely Jacobs, now liv-

ing near Murfreesboro, was my bunkmate, and he was
suspicious of my case, and kept me hid from the
doctor. Stokely says that I was delirious for two
days, and climbing up and down the bunk. When I
came to myself, I was out calling the roll of the ward.
I noticed that my hands were badly pimpled, but as we
did not have a mirror I could not see my face. Before I finished the roll call along came Dr. Burchard,
one of the prison surgeons. I have often wondered if
this was the Dr. Burchard, author of "Rum, Roman-
ism, and Rebellion," that helped dig the political grave
of Mr. Blaine. The Doctor looked at me and said:
"Toney, you have the smallpox." "No, Doctor," I
replied; "I have had a case of varioloid, and the fever
has left me, and I cannot communicate smallpox to the
other prisoners; besides, Doctor, let me show you";
and I pulled off my coat, rolled up my sleeve, and
exposed a perfect scar. "Now you know, Doctor, that
I have not got the smallpox." He said that I was not a
physician and not competent to diagnose my own case,
and that I must go at once, without further parleying.

The cold was below zero, and the hospital was across
a little lake inside the prison walls, and the patients
were in A tents—*i. e.,* tents shaped as the letter A, and
having a capacity of three patients each. I walked
across the lake on the ice, and commenced my search at
the head of the row of tents, trying to find some bedfellows who had as light an attack as mine. Nearly all
the tents were filled with patients who had the conflu-
ent type, but finally I found a tent with two patients—
one very bad and the other lighter—and I crawled in.

We did not see a doctor while there, but once a day a waiter brought us some tea and bread. As the hospital was some distance from the cook house, and the weather below zero, the tea was cold when it reached us. My bedfellows could not eat or drink anything, and I had all the rations, yet I could not get enough. The second night one of our bedfellows died, and all the vermin came to us, and we had plenty of company. The vermin will leave a body as soon as it gets cold. We had about eight blankets, but could not keep warm; and to make the situation worse, the men who died were dragged out and left in front of the tents, and in whatever position a man was when death overtook him in that position he froze. Some with arms and legs extended presented a horrible sight.

On the 29th of January, so my diary reads, I was ordered to the cook house for a bath, and my nice suit of gray was burned; and as the authorities did not keep any uniforms of gray, I donned a suit of blue, so in the picture I do not resemble "the boy in gray." I buttoned up my coat and was feeling comfortable as "the boy in blue," when the sergeant, who was robing me, took out his knife and commenced to cut off my skirt. "Hold on, sergeant," I said; "don't disfigure my uniform in that manner." He continued to cut until my skirt was gone, and then replied: "If I had left that frock intact, you might have walked out as one of our guards." And I guess I would have attempted it.

The fever had left my eyes in bad condition, and I went to the sutler and bought a pair of green-goggle spectacles, which materially changed my appearance; so when I reached Ward Thirty-six I jumped in the door and yelled, "Attention!" The boys quickly fell in line, hats in hand, thinking I was the Federal sergeant on an inspection. As I started down the center to inspect the line they grabbed and hugged me, for when

FROM SMALLPOX HOSPITAL.

I left for the hospital many thought that they would not see me again, because they had heard of so many deaths there.

Whenever there was any news favorable to the Federals, it was bulletined on the inside; but of course the unfavorable news we did not hear. So on April 10,

1865, was bulletined the surrender of General Lee. On referring to my diary on April 10, 1865, I find: "This is a dark day for us, and the officers celebrated by getting drunk."

As it is well known, the surrender took place at Appomattox Courthouse April 9, 1865, and the capit-

SURRENDER OF GENERAL LEE.

ulation papers were signed in the McLean homestead the next day. General Grant was accompanied by two of his staff and General Lee by Colonel Marshall, of his staff, and in the picture General Lee is in the act of signing the papers. The McLean homestead is about ten miles from where I was born, and some years ago a Northern capitalist bought the house, tore it down, and intended to transport it to Chicago to become an adjunct to the old Libby prison as a war museum; but the Libby prison venture failed, as it should have failed, and the McLean homestead at last accounts was in Appomattox, packed in sections ready for transportation to Chicago. I will say here that the Libby prison erected at Chicago was intended not so much as a monument to the inhumanity of the Southern people as it was to fill some enterprising citizens' pockets with the shekels.

I read from my diary previous to the surrender of General Lee that I saw a number of prisoners at headquarters making application to take the oath; these men were called "oath-takers," and they were ostracized by the men who were standing by their convictions of right. We had more respect for the men who stood guard over us than for these oath-takers. They were the men who reported to the commandants of the prison any infractions of the rules, thinking thereby to gain favor with the Federal authorities; but they were mistaken, because Colonel Beall, Major Colt, Captain Brady, and Major Richmond, Federal officers of the prison, had very little respect for them, and very properly so.

Referring to my diary April 15, 1865, I find this: "This has been another dark day for us. About eight o'clock in the morning the news flashed through the prison, 'President Abraham Lincoln assassinated by a Rebel.'" Immediately after hearing this, one indiscreet prisoner yelled out, "It is a good thing; old Abe ought to have been killed long ago!" The guards immediately rushed on him, and I thought that he would get the bayonet; but they trotted him to the headquarters of Colonel Beall, who ordered him tied up by the thumbs. This is a very cruel mode of punishment. A man is tied by the thumbs and pulled up till he is on his

TIED UP BY THE THUMBS.

tiptoes, and there is no way to relieve the pressure. If he tries to relieve the thumbs, the toes get it; and if the toes are relieved, the thumbs are in trouble. In a very short time he will faint, and is then cut down.

April 15, 1865, appeared as if pandemonium had broken loose; the guards were excited, and we did not know but that some of us would get shot or the bayonet.   No one sympathized with the fellow tied up, because he jeopardized so many lives.   I believe the artillery would have been turned on us but for the guards who were stationed throughout the camp. Looking back to the scene, I believe it very unfortunate for the South that President Lincoln was assassinated.   I do not believe we would have had the five years of carpetbag rule and other troubles incident to the reconstruction policy adopted by the government. I believe President Lincoln would have said: "The South has made a mistake in secession; and you have not seceded, because you cannot draw an imaginary line separating this country.   We are Americans; let us be friends and brothers again."

Of course we were uncertain as to our fate, and would have felt easier if President Lincoln rather than President Johnson had been guiding the affairs of the nation, for the reason that we knew President Johnson hated and had no use for Rebels or, as he called them, "secessionists."   However, on our return home we had the pleasure of meeting him, and to know him was to love him; and before he was elected to the United States Senate he had won many friends, who at one time had cordially hated him.   Once upon a visit to Greeneville, Tenn., I went from the little, insignificant tailor shop of A. Johnson to the handsome monument on the hill, and I thought of the possibilities of the American youth.

On April 24, 1865, we had sergeant's call, and upon assembling at headquarters directions were read from the Secretary of War to furnish:

1. A list of those who were citizens.

2. The names of those who had made application to take the oath of allegiance previous to the surrender of General Lee.

3. A list of those who had not made application to take the oath.

4. A list of those who refused to take the oath of allegiance.

In making out the list of my ward, No. 36, I gave the names of seven who refused to take the oath. In regard to the first order, with reference to citizens, many prisons contained citizens who were called "butternuts," who sympathized with the South, and sometimes uttered treasonable sentiments.

On May 24, 1865, a new form of oath was received in camp, to which all must subscribe before leaving. This delayed the release of the boys.

On June 7, 1865, my diary reads: "The New York *Herald* says: 'Orders will soon be issued to release all prisoners below the rank of major who will take the oath of allegiance.'" On June 8, 1865, orders were received to release all privates who would take the oath. The prison rules were now relaxed, and visitors could come and go with all liberty; and the prison was kept pretty lively in the daytime, and the boys did a fine business selling rings and other trinkets, and took in quite a lot of shinplasters and five- and ten-cent pieces of silver.

There were twenty-eight men who hesitated about taking the oath. They felt that they would perjure themselves, as they had taken the oath of allegiance to the Southern Confederacy. The month of July was near, and there were two hundred and fifty-one sick prisoners in the hospitals who could not be moved and were not in condition to take the oath. Colonel Beall was anxious to close the prison, and we asked him what he would do with the twenty-eight who

HOMEWARD BOUND.

refused to take the oath. He said that he would send us to Dry Tortugas to die of yellow fever. About that time I received a letter and money from Judge Whitworth, and the letter said that I had better come home and go to work, and I had begun to think before the letter came that it would be the best thing to do. So the twenty-eight subscribed to the oath, and were at the depot waiting for the train when an enterprising photographer set up his camera and said: "Boys, you should take a picture home to show the folks how you looked the day you got out of prison. I will

charge you only a quarter." I told him to fire away.
I was the only one of the twenty-eight that had a
quarter, and I took the center of the group. I was
clad in a light hat and a linen duster. After getting
out of prison I first went to a restaurant and then to a
clothing store, and fixed myself for traveling. I got
a shave also, the first one in many months.

The effect of the prison diet can be seen in the faces
of the men. One has lost his teeth and has his jaw
tied up with a rag, another is as pale as a ghost, and
several of them are very dark. One poor fellow can
be seen on the right with a blanket twisted and thrown
around him; he is too weak to stand, and is sitting
down. The bad effect produced on the men is called
scurvy, and is caused by eating salt pork. I am standing in the center, and weighed about one hundred and
eighty pounds. If the tintype picture would show
color, I would appear as rosy as a young lady. Colonel
Beall had given me transportation to Louisville for
each of the boys, and I said: "Boys, you must keep
close to me; if you straggle off, you will have to walk
home." The Big Four had not then been completed
to Cincinnati, nor the Louisville and Nashville from
Cincinnati to Louisville, so we had to go via Indianapolis, at which point we missed connection, and I
took the squad around the city sight-seeing.

There were many of the boys in blue with guns.
It appeared to me as an army post. As we were
strolling a squad of Union soldiers, recognizing us as
the boys in gray, commenced singing, "Hang Jeff
Davis on a sour apple tree." As we approached they

continued to sing, and I yelled out, "Why not hang some of the privates?" They replied with an oath that they would hang us, and started toward our group, when I said: "Come on, boys; it is train time." And we did not get hanged.

It can also be noticed in the picture that one of the

SURVIVORS OF CO. B, ROCK CITY GUARDS.

boys had captured a blue army vest, over which he wears a gray coat. Another one has a cotton haversack supported by a cotton string, to which is attached a tin cup. He is supposed to be on the lookout for buttermilk, coffee, or probably something stronger. The old slouched hats that had seen hard service were

quite noticeable. The picture is unique and antique—
unique as the only one ever taken of the group, and
antique in being over forty years of age.

Here is another picture over forty years of age,
the survivors of Company B, Rock City Guards, tak-
en in August, 1865. Where are the one hundred and
four who marched out so gayly from the old Academy
in 1861, when the bands were playing "The Girl I
Left Behind Me"? Seventy-two of them had filled
soldiers' graves; thirty-two had returned to their
homes; and in August, 1865, they were much scattered, and we could get together only seventeen, who
are herewith produced.

CHAPTER XI.

The Privations of a Citizen.

On reaching home we found change written upon everything. During our four years and three months' absence the city government was in control of aliens or carpetbaggers who ground out checks and bonds with a lavish hand. After paying my last fifty cents for dinner at the Commercial Hotel, I borrowed five cents from a friend, and proceeded across the ferry, which was just above the Louisville and Nashville Railroad bridge. I trudged along the White's Creek pike and finally stopped and tried to locate myself. When I left home, the whole country around Edgefield was a vast forest of large poplars, sweet-gum, hackberry, hickory, and walnut. There never was a country that produced such fine and diversified timber as this. It was all gone, and the stumps dug up. I looked for the old homestead, and found a dilapidated house that resembled it; the weatherboarding had been stripped off for some distance, and not a piece of fence was in sight. The trees my mother planted in 1845, the year before she died, were all gone. I walked near the old house, where some mulatto children were playing on the porch. I stopped to look at them, but could not recognize them. Presently a white woman came out on the porch, and I said, "Who are you?" She replied, "I am Jim's wife." I saw at once that she was a Northern woman. The

"Jim" she had reference to was one of my former faithful slaves. As soon as I got one dollar and twenty-five cents, I went before Mr. R. McPhail Smith and took the amnesty oath, and Jim and his wife had to vamoose the ranch. I trudged along for four miles farther to the home of Judge Whitworth, on the Brick Church turnpike, which I reached early in the evening. The family were all glad to see me; and after supper, feeling very tired, I went to the office room to bed, but could not sleep. Man is a creature of habit, and I had been so used to sleeping on a hard surface that I got up, took a quilt, and slept well in the front yard under the apple trees. James, George, and Leonard followed me, and it was nearly a month before I got used to a bed.

After helping on the farm for a month I came to the city and went to work for the Express Company. No one who had participated in the war on the Southern side could vote. In order to vote, a man had to subscribe to an oath that he had not aided, abetted, or sympathized with secession. Of course that disfranchised nearly all of the whites, and no one could vote save carpetbaggers and the colored population. Those who had real estate at that time, in addition to the city, county, and state tax, had a special tax to pay on the Edgefield and Kentucky and the Tennessee and Pacific Railway. So we had taxation without representation. The city was in the hands of a military post and metropolitan police; the railroads were United States military roads, and were managed by superintendents. It took nearly the entire police force to look after the lawless soldiers, who would rob and in some instances murder inoffensive citizens. We had no law or order; everything was in a chaotic state. In the meantime the Kuklux Klan and Palefaces were a law unto themselves. The object of the Kuklux Klan was a laudable one. It was to intimidate the evil doer and to protect the weak against the strong. No one knew who the Grand Cyclops was unless he recognized his voice in the giving of the oath, as it was administered in a deep guttural voice, and with hoodwink. The Palefaces were auxiliaries of the Kuklux, and were composed of young men who were too young to go in the war of 1861. Any Kuklux could join the Palefaces. Their mode of initiation was quite tragic. A large tent was in the hall room, and a sentinel paced to and fro; near by was a gallows, and before the initiate was to be hanged there was a terrible scuffling and firing of pistols. This was done to try the mettle of the young candidate. The Kuklux ceremony was quite tame compared with that of the Palefaces. The Kuklux Klan were supposed to have been tried by the fires of battle, and no other kind of firing was required in their initiation. I recollect five meeting places: in the powder magazine of Fort Negley; Masonic Temple; under the Olympic Theater; a store on Market Street; and over Evans, Fite, Porter, and Company's store. Those serving as Grand Cyclops were Player Martin, E. R. Richardson, Frank Anderson, Captain John W. Morton; and Judge J. H. Hales, of the Palefaces. There were about four thousand of the Kuklux and Palefaces in the city and county. Each Klan had a Grand Cyclops, but many of their names I have forgotten. I never heard of a large procession of Kuklux riding through our city intimidating the metropolitan police. There were some eighteen in the squad, and they were not trying to intimidate the police. On the other hand, I have always thought that the Kuklux Klan were auxiliaries to the police in suppressing crime. Columbia and Pulaski would sometimes have a horseback procession of one hundred and fifty or two hundred horsemen, the men all heavily gowned and the horses' hoofs muffled; and they presented quite a weird troop as they noiselessly marched through the towns, which would strike awe to the evil doers. It was not done especially to intimidate the blacks, but whites as well, if guilty of wrongdoing. The blacks who behaved themselves had the best of friends in the Kuklux Klan. I never heard of but two deeds of violence in our community during the existence of the Klan. One was that of a white man who was mistreating his wife. The Klan to which Captain P. M. Griffin belonged took the man out, gave him a good whipping, and sent him home. The man afterwards always behaved himself, and I think he died a good citizen. The Klans were located in all parts of the city and country, and kept up with their neighbors' doings. When a man was doing wrong a note saying "Beware," and signed "Kuklux Klan," was enough. The fellow's guilty conscience would say, "I am the man," and thus a reformation in his conduct would take place. So I have always maintained that the Klans were great conservators of law and order. The next deed of violence was the case of Mr. Barmore, of Indianapolis. It was said that Governor Brownlow had offered a large reward to any one who would ferret out the Klan, and Mr. Barmore came to Nashville. He soon called at the Express office for a package, and I asked for identification, and he brought in Mr. Sparling, who was at that time agent for the Knickerbocker Life Insurance Company. Mr. Barmore would have attracted attention anywhere. He was a man of fine physique, and dressed very conspicuously for a detective. He wore a fur cap, velvet jacket and trousers, high-top patent leather boots with trousers stuffed in bootlegs, and carried under his arm a large silver-mounted cane. After his first introduction he frequently called at the office for packages, and talked with me, but never mentioned the Kuklux Klan, although he knew that I had been in the Confederate army. One day he went to Columbia, and the Klan gave him a mock and asked him not to come to that section any more. A few weeks later he was in Pulaski, but did not get any information, and left on the train for Nashville. The Pulaski Klan wired Columbia: "Barmore is on the train." Four men in Columbia bought tickets to Godwin, and took seats near Barmore. I think Pitts Brown was the conductor. Just before Duck River bridge was reached one of the men pulled the bell cord and said to Barmore: "We want you." They carried him below the turnpike bridge, put a rope around his neck, and, notwithstanding his plea for mercy, they deposited his body in Duck River.

In 1870 our franchise was restored while D. W. C. Senter was Governor, and the Kuklux Klan was disbanded forever.

Another great privation, and I shall have finished.

On December 4, 1868, I was returning home from Cincinnati on the steamer *United States.* It was a cold, stormy night, and there were thirty barrels of coal oil on the bow. At 11:20 the *America* collided with our steamer, knocking a large hole in the bow, igniting the coal oil, and the vessel commenced to burn and sink at the same time. We had a large passenger list, one hundred and thirty of whom were lost. As soon as I felt the shock of the collision I rushed up to the hurricane roof to see what had struck our boat. I saw the *America* standing out between us and the shore, and there was no sign of fire about her except the lights from the cabin. From the light of our fire I read her name distinctly. I ran at once to the ladies' cabin and said to James W. McFerrin and wife: "Get out on the guards quick; the *America* will save us." I then hurried back to my stateroom, which was near the office, to get my watch and money. When I came out of my room, the vessel was afire from stem to stern, and on account of the dense coal-oil smoke I came near suffocating, and had to crawl some one hundred and fifty feet to the ladies' cabin, where all was in great confusion. Mothers were calling for husbands and children, husbands shrieking for wives and children. In all my privations in life I have never witnessed such a heart-rending scene, and I was powerless to aid any one. When I reached the outer guard, aft of the wheel-house and near where I left Mr. McFerrin and wife, the bow of the *America* was passing by, and the fire was nearly to the top of her chimneys. I started to jump on the stageplank space, but all around were burning piles of baled hay. As soon as her bow passed

I took a plunge, and went down, I suppose, about twelve feet; and when I struck the bottom, I shot up like a rocket, and struck out for the shore, which I soon reached. But I got very cold when a few feet up the bank, and could go no farther. I had on nothing but my underclothes, and but for a flatboatman who carried me on his back about two hundred yards to the burning *America,* I believe I would have succumbed to the cold. On my berth that night was my Baltimore overcoat, which I had worn in General Lee's army and had sent to relatives in Virginia before the Wilderness campaign. My relatives had forwarded it to me at Nashville in the fall of 1865, and it was lost in that terrible holocaust; but I was glad to get out.

I was sick for quite a while after the wreck, and the doctor said that one of my lungs was involved; but I said, "Doctor, I am too young a man to give up so early;" and I have been leading an active life to this date (December 3, 1906).

CHAPTER XII.

A United Citizenship.

When the reconstruction of the Southern states had been accomplished by our representatives taking their seats in the halls of legislation, we felt that we were again a part of this great nation. The South then started on an era of prosperity; it was not the new South, but the old South, with new life infused into it. We had been slaves to our slaves, and now we were freemen, as the yoke of slavery had been lifted from our necks. Whatever of bitterness had been felt was fast disappearing; in fact, there was always less prejudice between the men who fought each other than by the noncombatants of both sides. Between the old soldiers it was as with the schoolboys —one a stalwart, the other a weakling—engaging in a fight. The stalwart overpowers the puny one, and feels sorry, and they make up, and are faster friends than before. Such was the case with many of the boys in blue, who said: "We fought you with all the Americans we could muster, and then gave bounty to all the foreigners we could get, and also armed many of your former slaves to fight. We overpowered you, boys, and are sorry for it." And you know sympathy begets love, and that is why the boys in blue, when we go north of the river and attend their camp fires, make us welcome guests. Some of them felt so sorry for us that they suggested that we ought to receive pensions, and when the matter was agitated in certain sections the bivouacs of the South were *unanimous* in repudiating it. We have condemned pensions, except in cases of disability, because it discounts patriotism; and a Southern soldier who deserted his flag and joined the enemy and now receives a pension is getting a premium on perjury.

When the Spanish-American War came on, the men of the blue and the men of the gray stood shoulder to shoulder, the sons of the men who wore the blue and the gray in 1861-65 marched step with step, and won the victory that made us feel proud that we were Americans. Our country was thus cemented as never before, and prejudices gave way to an era of good feeling throughout this Union.

I wish that every American citizen could have been with comrade S. A. Cunningham and me and witnessed the unveiling of the bronze statue erected to the memory of the private Confederate soldier over the graves of our two thousand two hundred and sixty dead at Camp Chase, near Columbus, Ohio, June 14, 1902. The history of the monument is as follows: Colonel W. H. Knauss was a member of a Pennsylvania regiment, and was badly wounded at Fredericksburg, Va., the wound being so severe that the surgeons said he could not recover, and he was unconscious for some weeks. He finally recovered, and after the war moved to Columbus, Ohio, and engaged in the real estate business. Soon after he reached Columbus he commenced to look after the graves of our two thousand two hundred and sixty dead at Camp Chase, four miles from Columbus. He found the graves in a common overgrown with bushes and weeds, which he soon had cut and the ground put in good shape, and asked Governor Foraker to recommend to the Legislature an appropriation of $4,000, which was made, and the cemetery was inclosed in a substantial fence. Colonel Knauss then got an oval stone which, I think, would weigh about two tons. On this stone he inscribed: "Two thousand two hundred and sixty Confederate soldiers buried here; died in Camp Chase Prison, 1861-65." He then commenced to send appeals to the South each June, and he called public meetings of G. A. R. men, the Daughters of the Confederacy, the Bivouacs and Daughters of the Grand Army Circle, and he put these combined influences to work, and for years has had each June a successful decoration. He then conceived the idea of erecting a monument to the private Confederate soldier, and he had all his plans made, and approached Mr. W. H. Harrison, a wealthy manufacturer of Columbus, and said: "Mr. Harrison, here are the plans for the monument. These men fought for what they thought was right, and were as much entitled to their opinions as I was to mine, and they died away from home and among strangers and foes." Mr. Harrison was so struck with Colonel Knauss's enthusiasm that he said: "Build the monument according to your plans, and send me the bill."

Therefore, on that bright June day was assembled a vast multitude of citizens, Grand Army men, and ex-Confederates. A special train was run from Charleston, W. Va., bringing the boys in gray and their families to the unveiling. We met and clasped hands

with Governor Nash and Judge Pugh, both of whom
had followed General Grant at Vicksburg. We were
accorded a place on the programme, and followed Governor Nash and Judge Pugh, and spoke in the uniform of Company B, Confederate Veterans, and did
our best to picture the deeds of the boys in gray. On
the platform with us were the Daughters of the Confederacy and Grand Army Circle. We could not tell
one from the other so far as enthusiasm went. We
did recognize them, however, from their badges. Just
before the service commenced Colonel Knauss came
to each of the Confederates on the platform and whis-
pered: "Boys, when the veil is removed from the
statue, I want you to give us the old-fashioned Rebel
yell." So we did our best, and the entire throng
appeared to enjoy it. We heard the Ohio State Band
play "Dixie"; we saw the Ohio State Guards fire a
volley over the graves of our dead; we saw the statue
standing out like a life figure. The monument had
two bases, each starting out on a side of the oval
rock, about nine feet high, joined together by an arch.
On the arch was inscribed "Americans": I guess Colonel Knauss did not wish to offend any over-sensitive
people by calling them Confederates. On the apex of
the arch was the bronze figure of the boy in gray. It
was typical of the Confederate private: the empty
haversack, the full canteen; the old blanket twisted,
tied at both ends, and thrown around the shoulders;
trousers stuffed in socks, and shoes well-nigh worn out.
He was standing at order arms, and his body was facing his Southland. When I saw this statue I thought
of William Stewart Hawkins, the author of "Behind

Prison Bars," a volume he wrote in Camp Chase. Many will recollect his "Letter that Came Too Late." He died in Nashville November 5, 1865, of the seeds of disease sown in Camp Chase.   His last verses were written a few days after the surrender of General Lee, and were written behind prison bars as he looked out upon the graves of the two thousand two hundred and sixty dead, who preceded him only a short while.   The lines were entitled "Defeated Valor":

> Sleep sweetly in your humble graves;
>   Sleep, martyrs of a fallen cause;
> Though yet no marble column craves
>   The pilgrim here to pause.
>
> In the seeds of laurel in the earth
>   The blossom of your fame is blown;
> And somewhere, waiting for its birth,
>   The shaft is in the stone.

CHAPTER XIII.

RETROSPECTION.

LOOKING back to the events of the past, I have often thought, "All things work together for good." But for the Civil War, we would not have had the remarkable scene between President McKinley and General Joe Wheeler, when General Wheeler said: "Mr. President, I drew my sword to help disrupt this Union; I want now to draw it to help cement it." And General Joe Wheeler was commissioned as a United States general, and became the hero of San Juan Hill. But for the Civil War, we would not have had a Sam Davis. But for the Civil War, there would not have developed in the South the noble womanhood that made our history so illustrious—a womanhood that endured so many sacrifices in giving aid and sympathy to the soldier boys that inspired "the thin gray line" to maintain the struggle against odds much beyond its strength. There should be many monuments in the South to our noble women. But for the Civil War, we would not have had a Henry Wirz, who went to the scaffold rather than tell a lie. But for the Civil War, I might not have been a Mason and the humble instrument in the hands of my brethren in helping to build the Masonic Widows' and Orphans' Home.

In a previous chapter I said that Major H. G. O. Weymouth, who commanded the Prison Camp at Point

Lookout, was a Mason; and the following correspondence will explain:

NASHVILLE, TENN., Aug. 13th, 1892.

Editor Herald, Boston, Mass.: While in your busy city a
few days ago, in looking over the *Boston Herald* I saw the
name East Weymouth (referring to one of your suburbs),
and I wondered if this town was any kin to Major H. G. O.
Weymouth, who commanded the Prison Camp, Point Lookout,
Md., back in 1864. I was a prisoner there. Major Weymouth
was a Mason, and allowed the Masons who were prisoners
there to make an appeal to the Masons of Baltimore for
clothing; and he distributed it to them. If Major Weymouth
is in the land of the living, I would like to grasp him by the
hand. MARCUS B. TONEY.

BOSTON, Aug. 17th, 1892.

MARCUS B. TONEY, Nashville, Tenn.

Dear Sir and Bro.: Yours of the 13th inst. to *Boston Herald*
read, and I well remember the occurrence as stated by you;
and whenever you come this way I would reciprocate by grasp-
ing you by the hand. I live at 15 Beech Street, Cambridge,
Mass., and wish to meet you at my home.

Yours fraternally, H. G. O. WEYMOUTH.

I saw Major Weymouth at the United States cus-
tomhouse in Boston, July 14, 1905, and had quite a
chat with him. I said if the South had gained her
independence it would have been a crime to have
hanged him for the shooting of our prisoners by the
negro guards, for the boys had transgressed the rules
by getting on the dead line or talking after taps; yet
all will admit that the offenses did not merit such awful
penalties. Major Weymouth said I was right. He
cursed the negroes, and said he could not control
them. He did all he could by relieving them from

duty. In response to my request for his photo, the Major sent one which was taken at Point Lookout in April, 1864, and the following letter:

15 BEECH ST., CAMBRIDGE, MASS., July 25, 1906.

Dear Brother Toney: Enclosed please find photograph. I was pleased to hear from you, and should like to have you

MAJOR H. G. O. WEYMOUTH.

send me your "Reminiscences" as soon as you complete them, as they must be very interesting to all the survivors of your acquaintance during the war. Occasionally some of our Southern ex-prisoners of war come to see me—one from Hayes's Battery, New Orleans, but a few weeks ago. When you come to Boston, don't fail to come and see me.

Faithfully yours,   H. G. O. WEYMOUTH.

I have also said that Major Henry Wirz, the Southern commander at the Andersonville (Ga.) prison, was a Mason, and cited the testimony of Mr. W. E. Oakley, of Nashville, Tenn. (who was a prisoner there from Ohio), that Major Wirz was not a cruel man, and performed the burial service over the Masons there.

The hanging of Major Wirz was very sad. He was tried by a military commission, or rather drumhead court-martial, the main charges being an effort to starve the prisoners, and also the issuing of impure virus with which to vaccinate them. In the testimony used to convict Major Wirz were affidavits from bounty jumpers, thugs, and coffee-boilers. So notorious had been the actions of some of these men in Andersonville prison that six of them were hanged by their own soldiers.

Surgeon James Jones, who was eminent in his profession, and a resident of Nashville for quite a while after the war, made an exhaustive report in regard to the sanitary condition of Andersonville prison. The military commission captured this report and mutilated and garbled it so that it was used in evidence to convict poor Wirz, though there was nothing in the original report of Surgeon Jones to fix the responsibility of the condition of affairs on the accused. It is well known that the prisoners fared better than the soldiers in General Lee's army, who in 1864 were reduced to a quart of meal, and sometimes to a pint, per day.

Father Boyle, the Catholic priest who attended Henry Wirz, said that on the night before the execution two men called and went into the cell, and he thought they came to bring a reprieve. After they retired he went to see Wirz, and was surprised when Wirz told him that the men had offered him freedom if he would implicate Jefferson Davis in a conspiracy to starve the prisoners. Wirz told them he did not know Jefferson Davis, nor had he ever received any communication from him, and he *would die before he would tell a lie*. And the poor fellow went to the scaffold as a martyr to the truth.

In order that my young readers may know what I mean by bounty jumpers, I will explain. They were mostly foreigners who came to this country, on a promise of six hundred dollars, to enlist in the army. To men who had not been earning over fifty cents a day this was a great inducement. After enlisting and receiving the money, they deserted the army, or jumped the bounty.

Now as to coffee-boilers. They were so called in the United States Army because they remained in the rear and boiled coffee while the other soldiers were at the front. In the Confederate Army we called such men stragglers. We could not call them coffee-boilers, because after 1863 we did not have any coffee.

These were some of the men who testified against Major Wirz, a class of men who were despised by the regular United States soldiers.

The Masonic Widows' and Orphans' Home.

Coming down the steps of Cumberland Lodge one stormy night (December 27, 1886), I said to Brother W. H. Bumpas, "We must have a Masonic Home in

Tennessee." He replied, "I will help you build it."
A few days thereafter we had a set of rules and by-
laws, which we presented to the Grand Lodge on January 27, 1887. Under the by-laws no salaries or com-
missions should be received for services. We showed
the Grand Lodge that our charity, scattered over the
state and assisted by the various lodges and the
monthly allowance doled out to the widow and orphan,
rather encouraged dependence and did not educate the
orphan and tended to pauperize the widow; that the
Home would be indeed a home to the widow and a
school to the children, and in this school the children
would be taught physically, morally, and intellectually,
and be prepared to take their places in the world as
educated men and women; and when they were able
to maintain themselves they would take their mothers from the Home, would set up housekeeping, and
thus remove these charges from the fraternity.

The Grand Lodge, by resolution, approved our plans
and agreed to give financial aid to the cause, and always contributed their surplus. The Home was organized and chartered in 1887, with the following as
charter members: Marcus B. Toney, William H. Bumpas, James H. Collins, Wilbur F. Foster, Ben Herman,
Edward B. Stahlman, William K. McAllister. The
County Register, County Court Clerk, and Secretary of
State remitted the usual fees.

One day while Colonel Jere Baxter was building
Baxter Court, I approached him and said: "Colonel
Baxter, we are seeking a site for the Masonic Widows'
and Orphans' Home, and Mr. Joseph H. Ambrose
wishes to sell his place near Maplewood, and as you

THE MASONIC HOME.

wish to know who your neighbors are, we would like you to purchase and give it to us." He looked at me a moment, and said: "I have just as good if not a better location in the Maplewood tract. Send your committee out and select, and I will make a deed of gift." This he did a few days after, and the property was deeded to the above trustees in behalf of the fraternity of the state. Noble, generous Jere Baxter! I wish he could have lived longer, to witness the fruits of his gift.

June 24, 1888, the corner stone was laid, Brother Grand Master H. H. Ingersoll officiating. December 10, 1892, the building was ready for a limited number, and we ordered two families from East Tennessee and one family from West Tennessee. June 24, 1893, the building was dedicated by Grand Master Henry A. Chambers, and there was a special train from Louisville over the Louisville and Nashville road bringing a large delegation of Knights Templars and ladies; and they enjoyed a splendid barbecue prepared by our wives, sweethearts, and daughters.

In 1894 the Home had increased to ninety-two members, and in 1895 to one hundred and thirty inmates. We had to depend on voluntary contributions from our members, and the assistance of the Grand Lodge, which was always generous, especially after the children had been brought before them and demonstrated their good training.

Our wards were from every section of the state; and in order that each Mason might contribute to its support and feel an individual interest and individual ownership, our directors agreed to make an unconditional deed of gift to the fraternity of the state, and naming the Grand Lodge officers as trustees. The Grand Lodge accepted the property, and the seven trustees who held the title of the property under the deed of gift from Colonel Jere Baxter transferred their rights by deed of gift to the Grand Lodge officers as aforesaid.

Since the opening of the Home, some two hundred boys and girls have been educated, and are now employed in Nashville and vicinity, and are proud of their *alma mater*. Six have married since leaving the Home, and seven mothers have been taken from the Home by their children and are now keeping house.

EDWARD WORSHAM.

In 1876 a bright, manly young man named Ed. Worsham was running out of Memphis on the Louisville and Nashville Railroad as news agent. We were attracted by the gentle bearing and urbane manners of the youth, and offered him the position of agent of the Merchants' Dispatch Transportation Company, Memphis, which he filled to the satisfaction of the company and its patrons.

Ed. rose very rapidly in Masonry, and in 1878 was Eminent Grand Commander of Knights Templars of the state. The Grand Commandery met in Nashville, May, 1878, and Grand Commander Worsham reviewed the parade from a stand on the Square in front of the courthouse. Near him were his mother and sister, who looked with great pride upon their son and brother. Little did any of us then think that he would so soon pass from us, as the following telegrams will show:

NASHVILLE, TENN., Sept. 8, 1878.

ED. WORSHAM, M. D. T. Co., Memphis, Tenn.:

I see the yellow fever is epidemic in Memphis. Take such care of yourself as your general good health may demand.

M. B. TONEY.

MEMPHIS, TENN., Sept. 9, 1878.

M. B. TONEY, M. D. T. Co., Nashville, Tenn.:

Yours received. I went through the epidemic of 1873 on the Masonic Board of Relief. Have sent my mother and sister to the country, and I propose to hold the fort.

ED. WORSHAM.

MEMPHIS, TENN., Sept. 12, 1878.

M. B. TONEY, Nashville, Tenn.:

Brother Ed. Worsham died this evening with yellow fever.

ANGEL S. MYERS.

NASHVILLE, TENN., Sept. 13, 1878.

O. B. SKINNER, Gen'l Manager M. D. T. Co., Cleveland, Ohio.:

Our Agent at Memphis, Edward Worsham, died there yesterday with yellow fever. His was a noble sacrifice to the cause of humanity.   M. B. TONEY.

SAM DAVIS.

I esteem it a great honor to have belonged to the First Tennessee Regiment that had in its ranks so illustrious a private as Sam Davis. His first education was from a pious mother, who instilled into his mind that truth was a divine attribute. His early school days were spent at his home near Smyrna, Tenn., and he was later sent to the Military Institute at Nashville to finish the course. While at Nashville the war cloud burst upon us, and he hastened to Murfreesboro (which was eleven miles from his home) and joined the Rutherford Rifles (Captain William Ledbetter), which was mustered in the First Tennessee Regiment May 10, 1861, and became Company I. Captain Ledbetter was one of the noblest captains in the Confederate States Army, and was devoted to his men. Though he was of small stature and delicate frame, yet I have seen him carrying the gun of a lame or sick private. Captain Ledbetter lived till 1906, and left but few of old Company I behind him.

Sam Davis was a soldier full of adventure. Camp life was too tame for him; he wanted to be on the picket line, or out as a scout, or in the midst of the battle din. In all our campaigns under General Lee and Stonewall Jackson, in which we marched some nine hundred miles, we did not get into a fight, but got ambuscaded on Cheat Mountain, and lost only a few men. So when we turned our faces toward Tennessee and Fort Donelson, Sam Davis felt, as we all did, that we would soon be in the fray; but delays previously mentioned prevented our getting to the Fort, and when the left wing of the regiment reached Shiloh Sam was satisfied that he would get into the action. He was detailed to guard ordnance stores; but, not to be baffled, he gave a comrade twenty dollars to take his place, and in the first day's fight he was wounded, but not seriously. He went into the second day's engagement, and succeeded in helping to drive the enemy to the river bluff. Many a soldier with Sam Davis's wound would have pleaded disability and gone to the rear.

At Perryville, Ky., Sam was in the thickest of the fight, and came out unharmed, though his company suffered severely. After a long, weary march through

Kentucky, East Tennessee, and back to Murfreesboro, Sam was in the battle of Stone's River. Our line of battle was only ten miles from his mother's home, and in the second day's fight, when the First Tennessee was gradually pressing the enemy back, he thought he would soon see home and mother; but he was doomed to disappointment, for the order came to fall back. General Rosecrans was also retreating toward Nashville, yet General Bragg did not seem to know it, and General Rosecrans took advantage of the situation and called a halt, and then moved forward. We retired to Shelbyville, and had not been there long before Sam's brother, John G. Davis, who was a member of Captain H. B. Shaw's Scouts, came and got Sam detached for duty with the Scouts; and in this service he was engaged when captured near Pulaski and tried as a spy, and hanged November 27, 1863. He was unjustly executed, as he was not a spy but a scout, and in addition to watching and fighting the enemy was getting recruits for General Bragg's army.

I think Sam Davis was captured not far south of Lynnville. Captain John Woldridge (the blind Confederate) was at his mother's house when Sam came to Lynnville and talked with Captain W., and the Captain recognized his voice when Sam spoke. A few days afterwards Captain Woldridge's mother said, "John, what manly looking young man were you talking to yesterday?" Captain W. replied, "Sam Davis." His mother said, "He was hanged yesterday at Pulaski."

When Sam Davis was captured he was clad in a Confederate uniform, gray, and over it a Federal overcoat dyed brown. In one of his boots, concealed by a false inside, were a number of letters addressed to persons in the South; also a report from Captain Shaw to General Bragg, giving the disposition of the Federal forces in Middle Tennessee, including General Dodge's troops stationed near Pulaski. Captain Shaw was afterwards captured and placed in jail with Sam Davis, but in giving his name said it was Coleman.

Among the documents found in Sam Davis's boot was one which General Dodge thought had been given him by one of the Federals; and the General assured Sam if he would divulge the name of the informant he would set him free. In reply the heroic prisoner said, "If I had a thousand lives, I would give them all rather than betray a trust." I am glad that the Daughters of the Confederacy have erected a monument to Sam Davis at Pulaski, and that it bears the above godlike inscription.

Mr. Will S. Ezell, of Pulaski, was a boy standing near the jail about noon of November 27, 1863, and he said Sam Davis walked between the guards with a firm step and noble mien, and mounted the wagon and took a seat on his coffin with the utmost composure. On reaching the scaffold, some one told him of the battle of Missionary Ridge, and he replied, "The old First Tennessee must in future do their fighting without me." The Federal chaplain, Rev. James Young, prayed with Sam, then removed his overcoat, the noose was adjusted, and the tragedy closed. Some weeks afterwards Mr. John C. Kennedy obtained a permit from General Rousseau, went to Pulaski, disinterred the body, and brought it to his mother's home, and it rests in the family burying ground. Mr. Kennedy also retained the boot, which is now in the History Building at Centennial Park, Nashville.

After the war Captain Shaw was very reticent as to his movements during the conflict, yet he was unstinted in his praise of Sam Davis and his many exploits in the field. On account of his association with Sam Davis, he became peculiarly attached to his brother, John G. Davis; they were to each other as

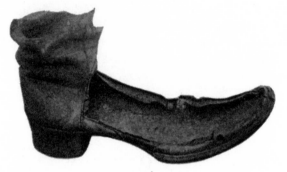

SAM DAVIS'S BOOT.

Jonathan and David, and owned an interest in the steamer *David White,* with Dan Kinney, of Nashville, as captain. The *White* blew up, February 17, 1867, on the lower Mississippi, killing John Davis and Captain H. B. Shaw and badly scalding Captain Kinney.

At the close of the Centennial Exposition at Nashville in 1897, President J. W. Thomas and Director General E. C. Lewis suggested and recommended that the History Building and the Parthenon be preserved, the History Building to be used as a depository for Confederate relics.

President J. W. Thomas was in the transportation department of the Confederate States in 1861-65, and filled that position with diligence and fidelity, as he

HISTORY BUILDING, CENTENNIAL PARK.

afterwards managed a great corporation to the day of his death. I loved him devotedly, and I learned from his secretary, Mr. T. B. Clarkson, that his last official act was dictating and signing his name to a communication to me.

Major E. C. Lewis was a boy during the war, and witnessed the Fort Donelson fight. His mother belonged to that noble band of Southern women who inspired the Confederate soldier to deeds of valor and endurance.

The History Building in Centennial Park contains many Confederate relics, and here may be seen Sam Davis's boot from which was cut the inner sole, disclosing the documents that led to his execution.

The Care of Confederate Graves.

NASHVILLE, June 11, 1902.

HON. J. B. FORAKER, Cincinnati, Ohio.

Dear Sir: While attending the unveiling exercises of the Confederate statue at Camp Chase, Ohio, a few days ago, I saw surrounding the Confederate Cemetery a substantial stone fence which I learned was built through your efforts, and I thought "one good turn deserves another," and would ask if at the next session of Congress you would introduce a measure appropriating $200,000 to suitably mark the resting places of my 24,456 comrades who were buried from Northern prisons in 1861-1865.

Yours very truly,   MARCUS B. TONEY.

The bill was introduced as promised, and was finally passed in February, 1906.

A few months after I wrote Senator Foraker I met him in the office of Judge H. H. Lurton, of the United States District Court of Appeals. Judge Lurton said: "Senator Foraker, I was a resident of near Columbus, Ohio, during the Civil War." "Ah!" said the Senator; "whereabouts?" The Judge replied: "At Camp Chase, where I was a prisoner of war. I went in as a private, and the Federals promoted me to sergeant of

SENATOR J. B. FORAKER.

a mess." Judge Lurton's case illustrated the possibilities of American youth—from a private soldier to the judgeship of the United States District Court of Appeals, and Senator Foraker before him to argue as chief attorney in so important a suit as the Northern Pacific Railway case.

Captain D. Jobe

was another intrepid scout who met a violent and sudden death. His family home was near Triune, Tenn., and his company operated in the rear of General Rosecrans's army, as did that of Captain Shaw. One day, after being hotly pursued by the enemy, he reached his mother's home and ran in and threw his arms around her and said: "Mother, I am very weary, and must have a little rest, yet I dare not tarry in the house but will go up to yonder thick woods, will get a little needed rest, and will come back and say goodby." Poor fellow! he never returned to his mother's house. Riding up in the woods, he dismounted, tethered his horse to graze, removed the saddle, of which he made a pillow on the ground, and soon was taking the much-needed sleep. The enemy crept upon him stealthily and shot him while he slept.

There was not a more gallant scout than Captain D. Jobe. All honor to his memory.

The Faithful Negroes.

So much has been written by Southern writers of the old uncles and black mammies of the South that one would think the field had been thrashed over. Yet there were different types of the old negroes, and many of us had different experiences with them. My mother died at the age of twenty-five. She was preceded by my three young sisters, and soon after by my father. So mother's maid became my black mammy, and the love she bore mother seemed to be intensified, and concentrated upon me. Sometimes she was cruel to her own children, but never put her hand on me unkindly. When I started from my home in Edgefield, clad in my uniform of gray and a big B on my cap, I called black mammy to say good-by. She threw her arms around me and said: "Don't let them Yankees kill you. I am gwine to pray for you." And before I reached the front gate, she plucked off her old shoe and threw it at me.

There was a superstition among the old Virginia darkies that to give good luck to those departing an old shoe must be thrown at them. (I will say here in parenthesis that the Southern children of those days imbibed some of the superstitions of their black mammies.) I don't believe my black mammy's old shoe had anything to do with my return; yet who knows but that through all the privations I have safely passed black mammy's prayer availed in my behalf? She lived to be fourscore and six, and surrounded by her children and grandchildren, seeming to forget them all in her last moments, she passed out with my name upon her lips.

When I received notice to appear at the photographer's in August, 1865, I said to old Uncle Ike, "My clothing is rather dilapidated." He replied, "I want you to look as well as any o' dem, and I'll fetch you down my broadcloth coat." And I am standing in the group of survivors of Company B, Rock City Guards, the sixth man from the right, and the best-dressed man in the group. Yet old Uncle Ike never thought of social equality.

Many negroes went with their young masters to the front as cooks and servants, and when freedom was offered them they declined, preferring to remain as servants rather than to assume the cares and responsibilities of freedom, which they thought might estrange them from their masters.

Company B, Confederate Veterans.

In explanation of my picture in the frontispiece I would state that in 1895 comrade William Aimison and I organized and recruited Company B, Confederate Veterans, to the number of one hundred, in which are represented some thirty-five Tennessee regiments, that took part in the war of 1861-65. I was tendered an office, but declined, and chose to enter as a private. I, however, was placed on the committee to name the officers. We were soon after attached to the National Guards, State of Tennessee, and wear a United States belt and cartridge box and carry Springfield breech-loaders. I suppose in an emergency call by the President or Governor we could muster sixty men for duty. Our first parade was at the Richmond reunion in 1896, and the next in 1897 at Nashville. Since then the company has been in parade at all the reunions.

We received an invitation to the reunion of the Blue and Gray on President McKinley's day in Evansville, Ind., October 11, 1900. Leaving here on the evening of the 10th, it was late in the night when the

Evansville and Terra Haute Railway switched our car containing seventy-nine men to the Fair Grounds in Evansville. We found four thousand Blues in camp, and when we marched in with fife and drum to the tune of "Dixie," there was not much sleep for the night. The Blues crowded around us, and we spun out war stories till early in the morning. Belonging to our company was Monroe Gooch, one of the faithful ne-

MONROE GOOCH, CO. B, CONFEDERATE VETERANS.

groes who went through the war—faithful to his trust. The Blues had provided A tents, each serving four men. The committee did not furnish a tent for Monroe Gooch, and I told him to crawl in with some of the boys, making five in one tent. Next morning we had dress parade at six o'clock, and as we wanted Monroe in it, we asked him to sit at the breakfast table with the company. Four Indiana negroes were cooking for each company, and I heard one of them say: "Look dar at dem Southern folks; dey knows how to treat niggers; one eatin' at table wid 'em." Yet Monroe Gooch never thought of social equality.

The Cleveland Grays, the President's Own as they were called, escorted the President to the city, but in the parade the Cleveland Grays were put aside and Company B, Confederate Veterans, given the post of honor; and the programme committee of Evansville citizens did me the honor to put me on the programme with the President, in an address to the Blue and Gray.

There was a large reunion tent in the Fair Grounds, and any one who wore the blue or gray ate and drank without money or price. After the parade, we opened ranks and clasped hands with the Blues, their wives and daughters. Four thousand Blues' to eighty Grays gave us a good many handclasps, and my right arm was tired for two weeks. We made a parade through the streets of Evansville, and had one grand ovation all along the line. I was gratified to see the city of Evansville decorated with so many pictures containing three in a group—viz.: Generals Grant, Lee, and Stonewall Jackson. At night Company B was entertained by the Cleveland Grays, and the only complaint I made was that they gave some of my men too much champagne.

It has been my good fortune to attend many reunions, but nowhere, not even in our Southland, have we met with a more cordial reception than in Evansville. The United Confederate Veteran reunions in the South are so largely attended, and so many have to be entertained, that it is difficult to reach them all. In Evansville we were the guests not only of the city but of the four thousand Blues camped in the Fair Grounds.

I think it will be proper to close this volume with some verses by Captain Harry L. Flash, of General Joe Wheeler's staff in 1861-65. He wished to go with General Wheeler to Cuba, but under the present army regulations his age barred him:

> You who faced the boys in blue
>   (When like a storm they rose),
> And played with life and laughed at death
>   Among such stalwart foes,
> Need never cast your eyes to earth
>   Or bow your heads with shame—
> Though fortune frown, your names are down
>   Upon the Roll of Fame.
>
> The flag you followed in the fight
>   Will never float again—
> Thank God, it sank to endless rest
>   Without a blot or stain!
> And in its place Old Glory rose
>   With all its stars restored:
> And smiling Peace, with rapture, raised
>   A pæan to the Lord.
>
> We love both flags—let smiles and tears
>   Together hold their sway;
> One won our hearts in days agone—
>   One owns our love to-day.
> We claim them both with all their wealth
>   Of honor and of fame—
> One lives triumphant in the sun:
>   And one a hallowed name.

A few short years and "Yank" and "Reb"
  Beneath their native sod
Will wait until the judgment day
  The calling voice of God—
The Great Commander's smile will beam
  On that enrollment day,
Alike on him who wore the blue
  And him who wore the gray.

INDEX